W9-BGV-389

The Next Chapter
in the Evolution
of the Soul

Communications from Seth on the
Awakening of Humanity ~ Volume Two

The Next Chapter
in the Evolution
of the Soul

Mark Allen Frost

Seth Returns Publishing
San Rafael, California

Copyright © 2006 by Mark Allen Frost
First Printing

Published by Seth Returns Publishing
P.O. Box 150152
San Rafael, CA 94915-0152

Editorial: Mark Frost
Cover Art, Design, Typography & Layout: Mark Frost
Printed by: Technical Communication Services

All rights reserved. No part of this book may be reproduced in any form or by any electronic or mechanical means, including photocopying, recording, or information storage and retrieval systems, without permission in writing from the publisher, except by a reviewer, who may quote brief passages in a review.

Library of Congress Cataloging-In-Publication
CIP 2005928178

ISBN 0-9740586-1-0
Printed and Bound in the U.S.A.

Dedicated to my family: Carol, Allen, Joy, Marianne,

Paul, Margaret and Gracie, without whose help

this project would not be possible.

CONTENTS

CHAPTER 1

Dialogue: Purpose of the Book
The Physical World
Scientists of Consciousness
Methods
Dialogue: Co-Creation
Up to the Light
Probabilities
Time
Consciousness Units
The Personal Reality Field
Illustration: Time, Probabilities and the
Personal Reality Field

CONTENTS

CONTENTS

CONTENTS

INTRODUCTION BY MARK

The definition of dialogue is "to talk through." This is also a good description of mediumship or channeling as I have come to know it. Over the last three years of my collaboration with Seth, I have gradually learned how to simply stand out of the way and let him "talk through." For the most part, I have transcribed Seth's dictation into spiral bound notebooks: one for book dictation, a different one for personal messages, one for readings for family and friends and one for what I am calling the Dialogues. These short personal sessions, sometimes only ten or twenty minutes in length, I provide in the hope that you may sense the vitality, intimacy and clarity of thought Seth provided as he assisted me in creating his second book. I also believe they reveal the distinctive non-linear methods Seth used to bring the material together for this project. Here is one of the early Dialogues.

Dialogue - Diary Notes
4/6/04 9:25 am

Mark ~ *Was it your idea to use my diary notes as part of Book Two?*

Seth - *Yes, in a way. We are part of the same Entity. I am your Energy Personality and you are learning how to communicate with me. Now, the establishing of communications with the Energy Personality is the main feature of Book Two, so you can give your diary entries as a form of exchange and as a living example to readers on how to do this. Mark, the pieces of the book are coming together. You can see that it will have a different feel to it than Book One. You can see the progression from Book One to Book Two and you can even see how Book Three will be created. And Mark, we can use humor here. We have humor to share and we shall. As Beings of Light we will BE light and we will lighten up the reader as we do so.*

To reiterate: your impulse - idea - was from a Simultaneous Self of which I am part. You chose to act on it by remembering it, considering it and asking your question. Now you have chosen to actualize it by giving it energy. See how the probable becomes actual? You are using your free will in the moment to select from the infinite probabilities, those that you wish to manifest. Now All That Is will create that reality via your crystallized intent. Do you follow me?
Mark - *Yes, thanks Seth.*

I am also hoping that by reading these personal messages you can learn something about how to create a dialogue with your own Energy Personality. For me it was like walking in the dark for many weeks and then finally making contact with "something." Then it was exciting and even fun to search for and finally discover the link to The Seth Entity. That was the most important event of my life. I am still awed and grateful for my good fortune.

Before I present Seth's new book to you, I must describe the events that transpired between the creation of Book One and the creation of this current book. Cas Smith, the co-author of the 9/11 book, has left Seth Returns Publishing. She is no longer creating books with us as she is pursuing other projects. We at SRP wish her much learning and success in her activities, and we respect her privacy in this matter. Thank you Cas for your vital contribution to the new Seth material.

As you may discover on reading this book, this is uncharted territory, and so more questions will be generated than answered. I encourage you to join the discussion on our website, write letters or in some other way participate in this growing community. Contact information is at the beginning and ending of the book.

One more item: I feel I must speak to those who are receiving medical treatment. Please do not consider the material in this book as diagnostic or as treatment for any medical condition.

And now, may I present, Volume Two in the series

Communications from Seth on the Awakening of Humanity ~ The Next Chapter in the Evolution of the Soul ~

INTRODUCTION BY SETH

Welcome to our discussion. This present book concerns mainly two broad subjects: the Energy Personality and the Fourth Dimension or the Unity of Consciousness Dimension, as we often call it. Therefore it will be somewhat easy for me to ferry back and forth from one topic to the other, without having to explain myself to a great degree. And I will do just that. You see, I trust that much of this material will be already known to you, for you will have read my first book since my return, or perhaps you are a reader of my earlier works with my First Subject and you are now taking a peek at the new Seth books. Now we will certainly provide background information before presenting the difficult material. However, please note that I will often refer you to my classic texts that reside in bookstores and in libraries, if you should prefer more illumination than I provide.

You may notice in this second volume in our series of books, that we are utilizing different labeling conventions than we have in the past. That is for a very good reason: this volume DOES INDEED signify a break with the past in that The Seth Entity is speaking to you in no uncertain terms now. The Seth that I am - meaning a particular set of personality aspects expressed from the broader context of The Seth Entity - is laying to the side some of the attributes that you may have held dear to your heart. The reasons for this change are that Mark, my Third Subject, is a unique personality that I must use my skills to adapt to, in order for the transmissions to begin and continue. But secondly, I am letting go of some aspects that may have been counter-productive in my earlier discussions with you. I will not go into detail on this second point, as I wish to have it remain as a lesson for readers of my earlier works to learn. But I will say that where I may have been pedantic, I now strive to be precise. There is no time for flowery language that may not have practical utility with regards to your Spiritual Evolution.

Now for those of you who are new to the material, I simply hope in this volume to keep your interest long enough for you to try out the experiments on your own. As humans you learn by doing. This seems to be a hard and fast rule in your physical reality.

There is another group I wish to welcome to this current effort of ours. This would be The Seth Entity human counterparts. Many of you I am sure will recognize this material. Perhaps you will remember some of it as ideas you have entertained recently. These ideas may have been presented to your awareness within the last several years, to help you recognize your membership in this collective, and to help you to seek out these messages.

Finally, it is certainly my sincerest desire that ALL OF YOU who pick up this book, will consider and take to heart the ideas herein. There is nothing to lose in this endeavor but your anger and fear, and only loving understanding and courage to gain.

NEW EXPRESSIONS
OF THE SETH ENTITY

This is my second book since I have again been speaking to you through my human counterparts. The subject matter of this volume concerns your place in the non-physical reality. Another way to express this is that we will be discussing the evolution of the human Soul, just as we touched on in the first book, but we will be getting quite more specific. We will be using my good friend Mark's life experiences a great deal in this volume, as examples from which to create material.

As with my first two subjects, there are certain ground rules that Mark and I must obey to keep the connection. For example: he uses his free will to "call" me into his consciousness, so that I can make the adjustments to communicate with him. I have his approval for entering, in other words. When we are done with a session I will either simply disconnect, and Mark will notice that I have left, or he will give me a time limit at which he ends the session by reminding me that "the time has come." Then I will simply say goodbye and disconnect. I must mention that I have found this simple two-way communication is definitely an improvement. The information is transmitted directly from The Seth Entity into Mark's consciousness and into his computer, onto the written page or vocally channeled before groups of people and electronically recorded. There is much less room for reinterpretation or mistakes to be made, as you can well imagine, than with another human consciousness in the mix. So I believe this bodes well for our future books.

I would also like to add that these new books are for the benefit of all. I did not specifically slant the material toward the understanding of readers of my older works. Therefore it is odd that some of these readers seem to feel they are "authorized" to censor my new material. I have urged Mark to be loving and kind to these ardent students of mine. Everyone is welcome to participate in this new network I am forming with my early readers and members of The Seth Entity. This is critical information that you will need to take the next step in human development. I wish all of you good luck in this enterprise.

PREFACE

Currently you are at a culmination of countless years of evolution. The transition to the Fourth Dimension is at hand. The mass consciousness has created a highly probable potential for humanity to shed the bonds of ego and allow the Soul Self of each of you to shine through. As you can imagine, metaphors are clumsy substitutes for what is truly about to occur. In the words of your religious manuscripts, you might say that the people of Earth are about to be enlightened: brought into the light of Higher Consciousness. Whatever the terminology you wish to use - and I do not mean to spite any spiritual path or religion by not including their terminology in this explanation - you are all, my beloved readers, in for a dramatic transformation that will alter you fundamentally. Indeed, it will transform you down to the core elements of which you are composed.

This volume is one of techniques and experiments you may use to contact your Energy Personality and explore the Fourth Dimension. The message here and the message we will be attempting to convey to readers in future books, is quite simple: you are awakening to your greater self in this lifetime. The recommendations we offer here are for your greater learning in the evolution of your Soul. Now, in this moment, as you are reading this book, you can begin your private journey by acknowledging that these words have meaning for you. Listen to the variety of responses that come from within when you do so. Feel the loving acceptance that supports you on this journey. Recognize the countless other beings who are accompanying you. Some of them have been with you since the inception of consciousness into your world. You are not alone. You have never been alone. Those such as myself have been watching over you and guiding you throughout eternity. We welcome you and we accept you wherever you are in your Soul development.

The experiments in this book are designed to give you some familiarity with the Unity of Consciousness Dimension, so that you will not become disoriented when the shift occurs. The methods for conducting your experiments are given in as simple a way as possible. Everyone should be able to get beneficial results through consistency and a positive attitude. Instructions for creating a personalized Ritual of Sanctuary are provided, to secure your voyage through these unknown waters, and a return to your Third-Dimensional reality.

CHAPTER ONE

The Study of You-the-Soul

Dialogue - Purpose of the Book
3/21/04 6:23 pm

Mark - *Seth, I'm ready to do 30 minutes or so of dictation on the second book if you're ready.*

Seth - *I am here. We are creating a mental overshadowing as you suggested. Give me a moment. The Next Chapter in the Evolution of the Soul... As I have said, I like this title very much. Issues of the human Soul are seldom explored in your world today. In religion, yes, you have a one-sided discussion about the "historical" Soul, for want of a better word. The true Soul, if I may be so bold, however, is undiscovered for the most part in your reality. Now, in our book we will be scientists exploring the Soul. We will be presenting our findings to the readers in a... give me a moment... group effort. We will have experimentation - the heart of scientific inquiry. Indeed, we will be investigating the correlations between thoughts, behaviors and created realities. We will be so introspective that we will see well* *into the smallest physical constructs of which your reality is composed. In other works, I have referred to these minuscule elements as CUs - Consciousness Units. I believe I will keep that name for these writings. Yet we will go further than we have ever gone before (humorously) to prove a point or two about these communications. Our peer review will include scientists, artists, working-class people and anyone else who is interested in perceiving the fundamental organizing principles of their self-created realities. Forgive me if I take the lead. Let us put some words together...*

The Physical World

There has always been a physical world, that is, the world of your perceptions. The Universe is and <u>always</u> was, period. Therefore, why speak of scientific theories that explain the beginnings of the Universe or the endings of the Universe? Your scientists are so enamored with studying and labeling their perceptions in the belief that they are acquiring knowledge. Yet the scientist using the physical senses, can only by definition SENSE the physical Universe. In a sense, (humorously) this physically-oriented scientist is quite LIMITED by the physical senses, and by the crude tools used to study the Universe or any aspect of the Universe, beginning, middle or end, in your terms.

What good is it to know how many stars there are in the sky and how hot they are? This is only science's skewed perception of what a star is. In truth, a star is more like a potent <u>idea</u> than a fiery object in the sky. And what is the

2

sky; molecules of oxygen and other gases that in some way combine to create your atmosphere? You may answer, "Yes!" but I hope you are beginning to see my point here.

The truth about your Universe is that nothing is as it appears, at least to the physical senses. Your perceived reality is just that, a personal perception. It is a creation of your own making with All That Is. It is your interior Universe expressed outwardly in a divine creative panorama. Now I don't mean to pull the rug out from under you, Dear Reader, but your world has much more depth and meaning to it than your scientists can explain in theory. For your world - the air in front of your eyes, the ground beneath your feet, the various "inert" and living forms - is actually composed of animated spirit. In a very literal sense, you and your environment are "god stuff;" spirit made physical, the camouflage of All That Is expressing in infinite variety.

Scientists of Consciousness

Now in these explorations we shall approach our studies as Scientists of Consciousness. And we will certainly create new definitions for these two terms, for your current definitions are inappropriate for our use. Yet, you are comfortable with these terms. You use them often in your dialogues with one another. Every day you hear of a new "scientific" study that proclaims to the world that something previously declared helpful to humans is now harmful, and so on and so on. This aspect of scientific research to come up with new information that refutes earlier information is simply the nature of the beast; that is what it is supposed to do. Yet, when you find that your scientific community continues to reverse itself, well you might get suspicious as to what the scientists are truly saying in these pronouncements. I will elaborate on this point later in this manuscript when we speak of matters of control and submission.

As a Scientist of Consciousness you may look to the heart of the matter, and with your Inner Senses surmise what is the TRUE nature of the reality of your world. The Inner Senses, or what we will also refer to as *intuition* in these writings, are the only tools you will need. Telescopes, microscopes, or any sort of electronic technologies, will not help you in this endeavor. After all, these are merely aids to the physical senses, and so are amplifiers of data once removed from the source. Why not go directly TO the source, and use those tools that are the unobstructed Inner Senses of mankind?

And so our definition might be: "Scientist of Consciousness - one who uses the Inner Senses to perceive and study physical and non-physical phenomena to obtain Divine Wisdom." I think that will do nicely. Having said this, I wholly understand that the "real" scientists who read these words will no doubt be upset. That is a good thing. The feelings of disquiet and rising anger are what precede the uncovering of genuine knowledge in my system; when the ego is dispensed with and the Soul is allowed to shine through.

So this is a teaching, if you wish, a Seth teaching on the nature of true science. Dear Reader, I have come once again to remind you of these critical facts, these distinctions, so that you may wake-up and enlighten yourself to your worsening dilemma. Now I have described this dilemma in the first book and I refer the reader to that material if you wish more information. For this present manuscript, however, we will focus on experimentation, and the creation of the means adequate to ANSWER your dilemma, and save yourself from extinction.

Methods

As we examine the physical world of Third-Dimensional reality, we will borrow some practices from your scientific method and alter them for our purposes. We will have experimentation, yet of a specific type. The subject matter is your physical world perceived through your Inner Senses and your outer senses and your individual beliefs and ideas about what is and is not possible. The subtext here is concerned with your individual lessons: those experiences you were incarnated into your current existence in this timeframe to learn from and to add to the experience of All That Is. So as you conduct your experiments, it will be as a way to throw light upon the meanings of your life currently. Why are you on the Earth now at this specific time? What are the broader meanings of your activities in this life? These are matters of Soul Evolution. The answers to these questions may come in the manner of divine information from your Higher Self. Which brings us to a major point: as you proceed with your studies and experimentation, it would be wise for you to scrupulously document <u>all</u> of the outcomes of your activities. Now this may mean writing down in long-hand in a journal, or typing into your computer or speaking into a recorder. Whatever the medium, please document as soon after the activity as possible. And as you add to the information regarding your Soul Issues - the meanings of life for you personally - you may notice changes in your beliefs about the nature of your Personal Reality. And just as a scientist must alter the hypothesis when faced with find-ings that demand this, so too shall you, as a Scientist of Consciousness, of necessity alter your beliefs, ideas and im-ages according to the new information - divine information - you will discover as the products of your experiments. You are on the path to your enlightenment, in other words, and you are approaching your awakening in an organized and disciplined manner.

Dialogue - Co-Creation
5/4/04 10:40 am

Mark - The intuitive flash I just received, the hologram that we co-create our reality with other humans, life forms and even "non-living" forms just as we co-create with All That Is. Can you go further?

Seth - Mark, I sent you the little insight. All That Is is the primary energy source for everything in your reality. It drives each and every atom in your field of reality and all fields of reality. For this reason, when I say that you co-create with All That Is, I mean that you, as a human, participate in a collaborative effort of telepathic communication and creation with All That Is to produce your world that you then perceive in a linear fashion. Does that make sense?

Mark *- Yes it does.*

Seth *- Please add "with your physical senses." Indeed, your physical reality "appears" to have substance. It is the substance you give it with your thoughts. Now remember also that since all in your world has consciousness - rocks, soil, air, atoms - everything has consciousness, all participate in this Gestalt of Consciousness we are speaking about. So you can see that it is ridiculous to treat anything in your environment as "lower" than you, or undeserving of respect, simply because you have labeled it "non-living" or "not conscious" or "non-sentient." We will develop this thread further in this writing in an attempt to encourage the reader to have an ongoing appreciation for the life they are living on your beautiful planet.*

Up to the Light

I often use the phrase in these new writings, "bringing mankind up to the light." Some may wonder what "the light" might be. Let us discuss this topic for a moment as background information for those who may be new to this material. To begin, humans are born into the Third-Dimensional world with an amnesia. There are exceptions where the child retains the memories, but for the most part, the child is shielded from memories of the time in between lives, the time in the Home Dimension. Now in the Home Dimension you are supported on a wave of unconditional love that streams from the energy source for all of creation - All That Is. When it comes time to begin the journey into physical form, the memories of this loving state of consciousness are erased. You incarnate into the physical human body to learn your lessons, and if you remember how perfectly loving and supportive the Home Dimension is, you might choose to cut short the Earthly existence before the valuable lessons are learned.

The "light' then, in our discussion, is partly the divine light of Higher Consciousness: the memories of love and support you experience when not in the physical body. Now light is information - knowledge. You as a race are becoming more knowledgeable with respect to your spiritual or divine past, present and future. Divine information is being streamed into your Etheric Bodies via glands in your heads. You are waking up to your true state, your divine heritage as gods.

Now, this information may be somewhat "too much" for some of the readers of my old material to take seriously. You may be saying to yourselves, "Where is the Seth who spoke in intellectual terms and avoided matters spiritual?" My answer to you is that it is I Seth who is speaking to you in these physical pages within this physical book. And it is also I Seth, your friend from years ago, who is reconnecting with you on the subtle levels and helping you to recognize the urgency of your current situation as a Soul. It is my hope that you will be well-prepared for the coming transformation in human consciousness that has been heralded in these writings and many others in your country and around your Earth.

The Energy Personality essence can be many things, including both intellectual AND spiritual. In these writings with my Third Subject, I will demonstrate this to you for the sake of validity and to help you to relax into the material. Just as a teacher in one of your schools will present the material in different formats with a different emphasis according to the effects the teacher wishes to have on the student, I Seth now choose to transmit my urgent messages through a different lens, creating a different focus, a slightly different perspective for the reader, than I may have done in the past with my first two subjects.

This is, again, divine information you are receiving from a Being of Light. If you have trouble with the words "divine" or "spiritual," please note that my friend Mark here has similar concerns. However, he is allowing me the benefit of the doubt and is working with me even though I may use words that make him feel uncomfortable. I assure you that he is gradually beginning to understand the great value in acknowledging the meanings of these highly-charged terms. By changing his perceptions he is changing his beliefs. He is becoming more accepting, loving and confident. I urge the reader to follow his lead and explore the TRUE meanings of divine, of spiritual, of love and of confidence.

9

Probabilities

I would like to briefly cover the subject of probabilities, restating what I have covered in earlier books, and adding to the material with some new ideas that I hope will illuminate this current manuscript. Those of you who have read my many books from decades ago, know that I am quite fond of couching my explanations, lectures and the like, in terms of probabilities. Indeed, this concept is at the heart of the broader concepts of manifestation and Reality Creation. To review: in your Third-Dimensional system, your consciousness with All That Is creates multitudinous probable manifestations, of which those you choose to actualize become part of your Personal Reality, what we now call, the Personal Reality Field. You experience these chosen probabilities as manifested physical Reality Constructs. However, the un-chosen probabilities continue on their trajectories of development. They each have their own separate evolutionary paths, in other words, and continue to grow and develop along their own lines, much in the same way that your current life develops along its own path, one experience leading to another, and so on. This is of course, greatly simplified for your understanding. I refer those of you who wish further information on this concept to my earlier works.

Now to add to this idea of probabilities for purposes of our current project together - that of accessing the Energy Personality, facilitating communication with it and then under its guidance journeying into an investigation of the

Fourth Dimension - I will also be brief. The probabilities for millions of humans - in the West in particular - to engage their individual Guides or Energy Personalities, are currently very high. Many of you are about to enter into the primary life lessons you came to your Earth in this current timeframe to learn. These probabilities will remain latent unless acted upon. The purpose of this current work is to give you some guidelines as to how to accentuate the probabilities for your individual enlightenment scenarios.

Time

In a related matter, and again as background to this continuing saga (humorously), we can discuss the subject of time, a concept that is very important to those of you in physical reality, though not in the least important to Beings of Light. Humans make much of "time" as you perceive it. You believe that you are making perfect sense when you say to another, "I don't have time to do what I need to do," and you seldom see the inherent humor in such a statement, for you take your time so seriously (humorously). But I must assure you once again of the TRUTH about time. The truth is that there is no time but the moment - the present Moment Point. All else - all of the emotion-laden memories of a particular past and the excitement or dread of a particular future - are fabrications of your imagination. You create the added elements of past and future to format your experiences into something comprehensible to your Third-Dimensional, physical senses.

11

Now this truth-telling regarding time has great utility for you the reader. Knowing and ACCEPTING that there is no time but the current Moment Point - your Point of Power - can free you from any guilt or other negative emotions concerning events from your "past," and also release you from the needless dread of so-called "future" events yet to come. This moment of truth (humorously) in your current timeframe, while you are reading this book, is all you have. And it is from this Point of Power that you create not only your future, but also your past. I will ask you at points throughout this manuscript, as my student, to attempt to internalize this over-riding fact-of-life as a necessary basis for further study and experimentation.

Consciousness Units

To continue with this updating of my concepts, we shall cover the Consciousness Unit. Much has been spoken of my CUs over the many years since I presented the concept to my First Subject. I am flattered and pleased that many of you have taken it to heart and explored this potent idea construct. Yet for purposes of this current manuscript, I believe that I will simply give the reader a "recap" as you say, and refer those of you who require more detail and intellectualization, to my "past" books and the related material on your Internet, in libraries etc. Now, in this moment, as we create these words, I am presenting Mark with a hologram, allowing him to sense inwardly, the multi-dimensional nature of the Consciousness Unit. (*I did sense the hologram. Lasting less than a second, it involved an expansion of my consciousness followed quickly by a reduction or extreme focusing of my consciousness. The microcosm and macrocosm concepts seemed to be demonstrated for me. mf)*

Simply put, the CU is a model - a Sethian model - for the activity of Reality Creation at its most basic. We may speak of these elements as Awarized Energy subject to the control of human thought. These are basic units of creation we are discussing and we may summarize their activity in a few words: you create your reality out of Awarized Units of Energy - CUs - through your intent powered by your emotion. Again, in other forums you may seek out more intellectualized descriptions. But Dear Reader, it all can be reduced to this previous simple statement.

At its most basic, which is where you must be in these research activities, the CU is the leading edge in Reality Construction. This "edge" is that point in consciousness where you may place your intention and begin to create consciously. Co-creating consciously with All That Is IS the <u>object</u> of this research project. Now if you require a more in-depth description, you may read the previous few lines again while you are in a relaxed state. It is possible you will intuit a deeper understanding of this concept. There is much more to the printed word, in other words, than one can grasp in one reading. This work, as in other spiritual texts, can be taken to as deep a level as your Soul Evolution may permit. Words have power. The printed words in certain books have the power to spiritualize the reader and open them up to other dimensions. It has always been thus. This current book of mine is simply a modern example of a book having the potential to catalyze in the reader the awakening of the spirit. This is not an intellectual pursuit. however, and you will not find your awakening on the intellectual path. You may spend lifetimes intellectualizing and explaining away your lessons. Yet you may discover in a brief moment in time - in a fraction of a second - the personal meanings for you on the planet Earth at this time. This is my hope for you upon reading this book.

The Personal Reality Field

As the diagram illustrates, at the intersection of space and time, and within the context of probabilities we have just discussed, you are the creator of your Personal Reality Field. As you read this book, you are at once creating your physical body, including the eyes and brain that read the physical book that you also create. All is created in the current moment by you, Dear Reader. And so you are all artists from the time you are born, working with the natural elements to create your multitudinous Reality Constructs, the building blocks of your Personal Realities. Now this creation unfolds before you in a linear fashion. You create, as we have just discussed, a past and a future to "match" your current Moment Point - your spacious present. You are artists, but currently most of you are naive artists, in that you create your works of art - your physical reality and all of its trappings - without much planning or thought. Thus, you

TIME, PROBABILITIES AND THE PERSONAL REALITY FIELD

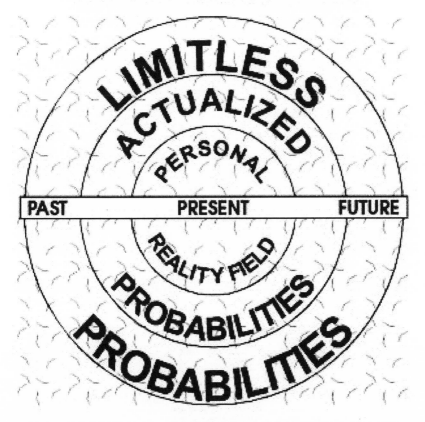

You create your Personal Reality Field by actualizing from limitless probabilities those Reality Constructs that support your beliefs. The white bar represents your Linear Time Illusion. The threads represent Consciousness Units, the elements of Awarized Energy that comprise all created realities.

~ Seth

perceive your reality, created unconsciously, as something separate. It appears as though you are at the mercy of your own environment, your world. The amnesia that I spoke of earlier helps to create this illusion of separation from your creative works.

Currently however, many of you are waking up to the true nature of your reality. You are questioning your personal beliefs and the mass beliefs of your societies. You are coming out of your amnesia and seeing the illusion of separation for what it is: a once useful fiction. As your consciousness is being raised and you are offered a glimpse of your true reality, many of you will take up the challenge to live your lives more honestly and more responsibly. Knowing that you are not separate from your environment, (you have made it) or from other human beings, (you are all one) you will begin to take actions that truly matter, rather than fritter away your time on the trivialities of egoic pursuits.

Fifty-Five Foot Radius

This Personal Reality Field we are discussing is simply the field of manifestation: the perimeter in your physical world over which your consciousness has the most control in the creation of Reality Constructs. The radius is about 55 feet for humans. This is not news however, as Beings of Light have presented these figures to humanity in recent years, and this information has been printed in books and transmitted along your Internet. This figure - 55 feet - is simply something to keep in mind when you are experimenting with <u>consciously</u> creating your physical world. You have the most control within this perimeter. Beyond 55 feet you cede manifestation energy and responsibility to other forms. Now, you take this with you wherever you go, this boundary of manifestation. So if you are driving one of your automobiles, and you are looking through your window, you have the most control over your creations within this 55-foot radius around you, including your automobile and your physical form. For you create your physical form - your body - and you create your automobile also, in addition to all within the radius.

I do not wish to go too deeply into this, as I will explain more about the manifestation of realities later in this series. Simply, humans have a 55-foot radius, and animals, insects and even rocks and trees have varying sizes of manifestation fields. Now remember that <u>all</u> you experience in your Third-Dimensional reality is conscious, from the material that makes-up your human eye down to the particulate matter that makes up the soil beneath your feet. Ponder this for a moment and I believe you will receive the information I am attempting to convey...

These limitations we are discussing are more a matter of the boundaries of the physical senses, than anything else. As I have stated in other works, there are actually no limitations to the Non-Physical Senses and that is why you can use the Inner Senses - which we will cover in later chapters - to contact and interact with beings beyond 55 feet and into other dimensions, across great distances and so on. The personal field of manifestation is related to the Third-Dimensional reality, in other words. When exploring other dimensions with the Inner Senses, there are no limitations. Your Personal Reality expands to the infinite. It is from an understanding and utilization of this fact of life that you may experience intentionally changing the greater consensus reality from your Personal Reality Field. As Mark just now reminds me, this understanding would support the validity of the concept of Thinking Globally and Acting Locally. In our third book, we shall have much more to say on this very important topic.

Dialogue - Creating Sanctuary
4/19/04 12:14 pm

Mark - *Last night I got the idea that the experiments are to allow the reader to individually access the various "levels" of consciousness. It will be different for everyone yet a common experience, in that we will all be accessing our Inner Senses, Simultaneous Lives, Energy Personalities. Will we have an experiment in contacting other non-physical beings?*

Seth - *Yes, and your thought that we must have a prelude to these experiments that describes how one creates Sanctuary and protects one's self from Negative Entities and influences, is a good one.* (Seth often picks up on my thoughts and answers my questions telepathically. mf) *Just as scientists must protect themselves from toxic, hazardous materi-*

als, you and our readers must protect yourselves from these negative energies when you are in the vulnerable states of meditation and during psychic exploration. This is a most important piece. It will be noted in the Preface and we will reiterate it before <u>each</u> experiment. You may also use the protection ritual before you get me. It is a good practice generally to do so. Now one more experiment - I just gave you a hologram - will be to have the reader "link up" with other Seth readers and create the SimeTime Salon that you spoke of in your introduction in the first book. See how the pieces fit together? (See Final Chapter. mf)

Experiment - Ritual of Sanctuary
Hypothesis: enacted sanctuary ritual seals off negative energies

Building on the exercises from Book One, this experiment will explore the means for creating a unique protection ritual for the reader to enact prior to psychic investigations. Now Mark, I just gave you a hologram regarding this experiment and it concerned the essences of protection that are individual images and feelings of security and peace. *(I did experience a flash of emotional intensity that was reassuring in tone. It included some pleasant personal memories from my early childhood. mf)* Each reader may for themselves list their beliefs and images of security and peace and then distill them down into a potent image or statement that virtually resonates with the energies we are discussing. Again, each individual will create a distinct image or verbal or written statement with accompanying emotional content. This is the Ritual of Sanctuary that the reader may perform before each experiment. It is a good idea for the reader to write down and draw pictures of the images and content they are experiencing for future reference. The ritual may include body movements or gestures, the cultivation of emotional states, visualizations of various types and so on. The reader may wish to try out the ritual a number of times until it elicits the desired state of Sanctuary, that is, a feeling of support as if one were a beloved child in the arms of one's adoring mother. Naturally, the reader may have different criteria for sensing ultimate protection.

One note here... the descriptive terms Emotional Body, Home Dimension etc. are, as Mark mentioned, simply for the convenience of the reader. Your reality obviously unfolds seamlessly for your perception. There are no distinctions between dimensions and your physical form, for example. All of our terminology is presented for your use in your Third-Dimensional reality so that you can make sense of this new information we are presenting. You are used to naming and so we will name in our material.

Findings - Document your findings. This may mean that you will write down the results of your ongoing efforts in creating a Ritual of Sanctuary that works. This is a personal matter. Only you will know when you have fine-tuned your ritual to the point that it assists you in creating the sacred space of Sanctuary.

Experiment - The Personal Field of Manifestation
Hypothesis: you can sense the creation of your personal reality field

Perform your Ritual of Sanctuary.

Let us attempt to help you get a feel for your own personal field of manifestation with an experiment. I would ask you to quiet your mind using any relaxation technique you may have gathered in your lifetime. Deep breathing, visualizing a restful scene and gently stretching the body are some ways to accomplish this relaxation. When you are relaxed, please look out in front of you and establish where in the distance your 55-foot limit might be. For these purposes it would help if you were doing the experiment outside. If you are indoors, you may be able to sense it intuitively. Now sense how this boundary surrounds and supports you. Sense also how the perceptive reality within this perimeter seems to be subject to your intentions. Now remember, you are collaborating with All That Is in this creation of physical reality. Can you sense how the creative power of the veritable Universes flows into your Reality Constructs and creates a seamless impression of "bedrock" reality for your physical senses

to perceive and experience? Can you sense the con-
nectedness between you and everything else? Every cell, each molecule, every atom is connected to
every other cell, molecule and atom. This is a literal
fact. Feel it, imagine it, act on it. In this way, you Dear
Reader are connected to everything, everywhere in
your Universe.

As you sense this power, can you see that all of
your created forms in your perception have their own
energy fields? Every atom has its own aura - the electromagnetic corona. Every self-created physical object has its collective aura. Again, here you are asked
to put aside feelings of low self-worth, guilt and fear
and experience the true nature of your being - as co-
creator of your physical world. Now this witnessing
of the true nature of your Personal Reality can co-
exist with your ideas and images from your religious
and spiritual teachings. One need not exclude the
other. Indeed, the most beneficial products or findings that may come from this experiment are the experienced moments of holding divergent views of
reality. For it is these glimpses of other truths that
may eventually, when you are prepared, convince you
to discard beliefs and behaviors that no longer serve
You-the-Soul.

Findings - Write down or in some other way
document your findings for future reference.

Experiment - Clearing the Emotional Body
Hypothesis: raising the focus from the emotional to the mental center clears emotional turmoil

Perform your Ritual of Sanctuary

This experiment concerns the creation of a personal perspective through which you may create and perceive your world with greater clarity. As a human, you are most likely in the habit of creating and perceiving your Personal Reality through the Emotional Center of the heart region. For our purposes, we will raise that focus of awareness up to the Mental Center, which has its physical counterpart in the head directly between the eyes. Sensing where the energies might be in your heart region, see what image or emotion comes from it. If you have an image of churning, as of emotions strengthening and dying out, you are on the right track. Now, using your intention or will, bring this churning energy up from the lower centers into the higher centers of the throat and head. As you do you may notice that the churning emotionality ceases. It may be replaced with a cool clarity and a feeling of relaxation. Keep with this feeling of clarity, purpose and un-emotionality for a few moments. Embody it, my friend.

Findings - Document your findings. This may simply be your observations, personal meanings, drawings etc.

Experiment - Meditation
Hypothesis: you can learn to connect with the divine energies in a purposeful way

Now… our form of meditation is quite simple. The goal is to connect with the stream of divine information, purposefully. You are already accessing divine information as you sleep. This experiment may assist you in creating rituals of contact and communication with the divine source through what we broadly define as meditation. First let me remind you that you will be encountering ecstatic states of consciousness. Your relaxed position in your chair, on your couch or pillow, will appear to others as though you are in an ecstatic state, and indeed you shall be.

Perform your Ritual of Sanctuary

To get a feel for this sitting posture, sit down in your comfortable chair or other structure with your feet flat on the floor. If the chair has armrests, rest your forearms upon the armrests or simply rest your arms and hands in your lap. Now the torso should be balanced comfortably on the hips, pelvis and seat. The most important aspect of this meditation position is this: the head should be resting on the neck slightly to either the left or right side. The head should be tilted back slightly, again, as though you were experiencing ecstatic states. To others, it would appear as though you were profoundly relaxed and content though not

24

asleep, not unconscious. You have one foot in the physical and one foot in the metaphysical domains. Now your intent is very important here. Simultaneously, as you create the relaxed body posture for meditation, you are focusing on creating the connection to the divine. This will be unique to the individual. I have described this as "embodying" the divine in this present manuscript. With your imagination you will use your powers of creativity to establish the "divine connection." You will know it when you sense it. The loving emotions will be quite noticeable - the wave of ecstasy just below the surface. As you notice this pleasant feeling, the divine information will no doubt begin to stream into your Etheric Body through the physical channel between your eyes. By keeping free from distractions, you may continue to "drink in" these energies for as long as you wish, though fifteen minutes to an hour per session is adequate.

Now this stream may cease on its own and you will come to Third-Dimensional consciousness soon afterward. Or you may simply have the intention to come out after a specific amount of time and you shall. Simply suggest to yourself that you will come out at a specific time, before you begin the meditation. It is also a good practice to not attempt an intellectual analysis of the meditation session immediately afterward. Give yourself some time. The energies will play out within your Etheric Body over time, and you really needn't try to investigate how you are doing. The positive changes that will occur in your life as you meditate regularly shall in all probability be enough proof that your behaviors in this matter are worth the time and effort. This is primarily a receptive exercise or experiment, in other words. You are allowing the divine energies of All That Is to wash over you, to cleanse and to heal.

Findings - Document the results of your experiments with meditation. After you have gained some proficiency, verify for future reference, what you feel and think during and after the sessions.

CHAPTER TWO

A Brief History of Humanity

Dialogue - Crystals of Atlantis
4/14/04 3:55 pm

Mark - In the first book I asked you about Atlantis and that civilization's use of crystals for various purposes and how I was fascinated by everything Atlantean. Can you comment on my personal connection to Atlantis, if there is one?
Seth - Mark, now I just gave you a response in the form of an image and a feeling tone as you closed your eyes briefly. I also instilled the word "bleedthrough" into your consciousness. It was a momentary, multi-sensory hologram...
Mark - Yes. I got it clearly. Thanks for that.
Seth - Now bleedthroughs can come from what you call your past or your future and also from contemporary existences - from all of your Simultaneous Lives. And your other point regarding crystals: some of your contemporaries are infatuated with crystals and ascribe great powers to them. These will be the ones who will incarnate or simply transi-

tion into the Unity of Consciousness Dimension and become the leaders in the new technology of crystals I spoke of in the first book. These are truly "crystal people" who may incarnate multiple times, in similar occupations, to consolidate their experience and knowledge.

(The hologram lasted a fraction of a second. I was compelled to close my eyes briefly and experienced a little bleedthrough. The vision was supported on this comfortable body feeling of ecstasy. The colors were pastels of turquoise and magenta. "I got it clearly," yet I cannot now remember it just a few minutes later. mf)

Lessons

You are born into physical form to experience a life of lessons. This means that although you have free will to choose from an infinite supply of probable actions, you will choose those actions that support a particular context - a dramatic background, if you will - upon which you shall project your reincarnational dramas, comedies and the like. Now you must pretend that you do not have such a stake in this production. You are, therefore, surprised when great blessings or tragedies occur on the stage of your life. But currently my friends, many of you are waking up to discover yourselves as actors on the stage, and you are acknowledging to yourselves that you are also the producers and directors of these enlightened stories.

To illustrate my point here, consider the tales of your leaders, your heroes and heroines from your historical past, as portrayed in your literature and your motion pictures. You can see the symbolism and meaning in the lives of these great leaders, can you not? Yet can you also see the meaning and lessons in your own ongoing lives? The heroic struggles of your ancestors are often embellished in larger-than-life terms through dramatization, this is true. Yet the symbolic lessons characterized in books or on the screen are of no greater importance in terms of the Soul, than the heroic acts performed by any of you in your daily lives. You are all heroic. You are all born into Earthly existence to learn your symbolic lessons.

Early Humans

Now let us discuss the origins of what is currently the six-billion plus humans on your planet Earth. Where did you all come from? There have been many explanations from your religions and from your scientific community on your origins. And in the same way that your religious leaders anoint themselves as the only purveyors of spiritual knowledge - including the story of the emergence of humans from the world of spirit - scientists, in their quest for power "over" the material world, have established themselves as the tellers of the "true" story, the "scientific" explanation for humanity's origins. Yet what your scientists refer to as the "beginning" of humankind is simply not accurate. Humans have developed from inception onto your planet into highly technological societies countless times, over countless ages, billions and billions of years if you are speaking of linear timelines. Until your scientists can conceptualize within these broader frameworks, the debate will continue to center on theories of early man, use of primitive tools etc. etc. etc.

The "early man" that I am describing, began life on your planet Earth with a highly advanced intellect and a capacity for creating technologies that eventually far surpassed your current efforts. Now these capacities or potentialities were invoked via telepathic conversations between these "early" humans and their higher selves - Spirit Guides or Energy Personalities. In this way, the current expansion of consciousness you are experiencing in your timeframe, is a repetition of other invocations of inherent capacities your race has experienced in a cyclical fashion over the millennia.

Created Histories

Yes, it has certainly been a fantastic voyage from where and when humanity has "begun" until now, your current Moment Point in this timeframe. Let us focus on the history of humanity I hinted at in Volume One of this series. Of course, this history I am describing is merely one of literally millions of probable histories. For there are an infinite number of probable realities one can create by focusing on them. The consensus reality then - the reality that becomes the agreed upon mass-created reality and thus the history of consensus reality - is that reality most of humanity agrees to create. Majority rules here in other words. As a collective of humans, you create in the dream state the essential frameworks for your Personal Realities that you will "cover" with your camouflage Reality Constructs upon awakening. Each of you develop from your personal reservoirs of memory and imagination, the evocative reincarnational environments and events that you experience upon awakening. It has always been thus. As I have said, beginnings and endings have relevance only in discussions of linear timelines. In truth, your lives are lived simultaneously, at once within the present moment. However, since time and space are useful theories to you….

Among the Stars

Your beginnings are among the stars. Do you not each of you look to the stars with longing as you observe your great Milky Way Galaxy? There are you origins. There in the stars are the origins of your races on your Earth. From your ancient tales of star gods seeding the Earth with human beings, to your "science fiction" tales of extra-terrestrial visitations, all of these so-called myths and so-called fictions hold elements of the truth about your TRUE beginnings. Now the ancient tales are often literal interpretations of what your human ancestors perceived. Literal. And your science fiction interpretations originate from your collective unconscious - that store of memory that contains all of Earthly experience past, present and future. Your authors and artists - visionaries - use this great store of symbolic truths to create their artistic works. Those of you who appreciate the

31

truth in those works - just as the aboriginal and ancient proto-humans appreciated the tribal stories - are experiencing your connection to the sacred via this collective Soul network.

When I suggest to you that your origins are among the stars, I am saying that within what your scientists describe as intensely hot gaseous spheres of energy- your so-called "stars" - are the "seeds" of humanity. But how, you might ask, can living cells exist in such an environment? The answer is, inter-dimensionally. Many interesting and productive life forms - some of which you might term humanoid and others you would surely not - exist and develop in dimensions within and upon stars and planetary bodies throughout the Universe. This is a fact. They are singularly perfectly suited to their dimensional existences. Therefore, I trust the reader may understand that travel from stars and planets and other more distant systems, to Earth or any other destination in the Universe, for that matter, IS a matter of inter-dimensional travel, and inter-dimensional travel is instantaneous.

Now previously in my writings with my Second Subject I spoke of the origins of humanity. I told you that you were indeed of extra-terrestrial origins, and this is quite true. Your Earth was seeded with human life forms from other planetary and star systems to populate the planet and to allow these life forms to learn from their experiences.

As you absorb this revelatory material - that your race has been seeded onto Earth from other galaxies, other star systems - you may shake your head in disbelief. It is a great deal to comprehend. As I have said, not only do you take on individual lives in material form for learning purposes, and certainly not sequentially within the same family "lineage," but definitely within different family organizations, of different races, in different sexual roles.

Now there is a great "forgetting," the amnesia I spoke of earlier, that masks your memories of past lives and Home Dimension experiences. This forgetting explains why you can speak quite honestly and ardently about your "heritage," and those in your family tree who have suffered, or perhaps triumphed in their lives, thus "preparing" the future for your accomplishments or failings. Again, this is your limited perception. As your Inner Senses become more acute during your awakening, you will <u>see</u> that you are enacting your reincarnational dramas within the Earth experience for spiritual purposes. And as an addendum - even though you may not "believe" in matters SPIRITUAL.

Inter-Dimensional Travel

To go "back in time" (humorously) even further in our description of your origins, we are presented with the creative source for all that we describe - All That Is. It is this divine source which spins off - literally and figuratively - parts of itself from itself, that become these incipient humans we are describing - these evolving Souls - you and your fellow inhabitants of Third-Dimensional reality on your Earth. So you are spun, almost as on a great loom, from the fertile essence of All That Is, and you are spun-off from All

That Is into your forthcoming life. In a sense, your beginnings are in waiting, biding time for years, perhaps even centuries within these star systems, until the opportunity for birth arises.

In terms of linear timelines, most of you who are reading this second book of ours, have resided in a few systems within the galaxies: Arcturus, Sirius and another complex your scientists have not yet discovered and named, and so does not yet exist, in your terms. Interdimensional travel is, as I said, instantaneous. One is at one moment existing in a dimensional plane in a star system far from Earth, and in the next moment one enters the physical body of a Soul - a baby being born on Earth. This is how it works, my friend. This is how it has always been done.

Now to repeat myself here, for I believe it bears repeating, your Soul Self chooses the life it wishes to be born into - the particular human baby born into its unique circumstances on your Earth. You are born to live a life of lessons, for your own education and Value Fulfillment and for the greater experience of All That Is.

Mystery Civilizations

As we keep to our linear timelines, the next step for your species was residence and development within several civilizations, some noted in your mythologies: Atlantis, Lemuria and GA, the latter a decidedly matriarchal society. These "mystery civilizations" as you call them, have been romanticized in your literature. The true stories, however, are just as interesting. We will touch on each of them briefly.

GA the Matriarchy

Let us discuss first the least known of these civilizations: GA, a civilization from your Third-Dimensional existence, eight-thousand years before your Christian era. This society spread over much of your European world and was governed by women with men in primarily administrative and physically creative roles. Many of you have passed through this civilization experiencing roles as males or females within this society that honored the female aspects of consciousness. The men created physical objects, built homes and other constructs. Now the men were not demeaned here. It was a different concept. Men and women were fulfilled in their roles. There was no "battle of the sexes," as you have currently. Cooperation was the watchword, the goal of all relationships.

GA, as we shall refer to this matriarchal civilization, was a society based on loving appreciation for one's fellow participants in the culture. In many ways, just as your American society is an experiment in multi-culturality - the melting pot - GA was an experiment in a society based on love. As I have just now related to Mark, the Sumari influence was strong in this culture. The language was primarily Sumari, a language based on love and unconditional acceptance of others, both within the family and outside the family. The loving essence of each person was noted, respected and cultivated in relationships.

Mark has recently searched for references to GA in books and on your Internet. He will not, however, find these references. Yet as time goes by (humorously), in your current timeframe, "discoveries" will be made by archaeologists and other scientists using their Inner Senses to guide them. These discoveries will lead to a complete reinterpretation of the historical record pertaining to civilizations from your perceived past.

Now it may seem obvious that some of your current legends regarding matriarchal societies came from the GA civilization we are describing. This is quite true. These colorful tales of tribes and full societies of empowered creative women enter your collective consciousness via bleedthroughs, just as described earlier in this manuscript. Because your future and past are created NOW, in your current Moment Point, individually and collectively, the full cellular memories of that civilization will be imprinted and "come to mind" when the probabilities for a matriarchal society can be entertained seriously in this present timeframe of yours. Do you see how it works, Dear Reader? You are the creator. Your creations are limited only by your imaginal and perceptual boundaries.

Dialogue - Atlantis Hologram
4/26/04 3:37 pm

Seth - *No you are not being a pest* (answer to my thought that I was asking too much about Atlantis. mf). *It is just that, the manifestation of Atlantis is indeed ongoing, as we speak. Therefore it is difficult to present the information in a way you could understand in your Third-Dimensional existence. Now I could send you a hologram, as I did earlier, with the information embedded in it. Would that be acceptable?*

Mark -*Yes. I like that idea.*

Seth- *Excellent. Then you may translate the multi-dimensional missive into terms your contemporaries may understand. Watch and listen. This may turn out to be a useful technique for our projects.*

(I went through the last part of my day on 4-26-04 waiting for the hologram, thinking it had not come. Then during the night I awoke several times with the multisensory image of numbers of people lying down on the ground, head to foot, in series, in a grid and somehow this generated power. Then the following morning I finally got it - that image is very much like a hologram of Atlantis, in that it reveals the fundamental power of the culture: they harnessed thought and used the collective power of human mentality - telepathy - to create their world consciously. This is where we are headed in the future if we utilize Seth's ideas. That's why he says Atlantis is partly in our future. I also received a related mes-

37

sage: Book Two is about networking from Book One to create the collective; literally People Power. Book Three will document the activities of The Seth Entity counterparts as they internalize and act upon Seth's new messages. mf)

Children of Atlantis

You Mark, have a great interest in the stories of Atlantis and other mystery civilizations. As a child, you enjoyed movies with Atlantis as the subject matter. You have read books on the topic throughout your life. You are drawn to this "myth" as are many of your fellow humans in your timeframe. There are reasons for this attraction. You are "children of Atlantis," in a very literal sense: "children," in that you have a tendency, as a species, to not want to learn your lessons. I am speaking of the spiritual lessons that you came to your planet to learn. And you are from Atlantis, that is true, a civilization that reached the highest station in technological achievement, only to destroy itself through misuse of these capabilities. This is of necessity a greatly over-simplified explanation, for Atlantis is as much in your future as your past, as I have said.

Now, as an aside, previously I have suggested in the 9/11 Book that humanity is indeed headed down the wrong path with regards to the development and use of nuclear technologies. And this is the arena in which mankind, particularly in the industrialized nations of Earth, will either go the way of the Atlanteans and cut short their evolution in childhood, or begin to make the right decisions as a loving collective and mature into responsible stewards as co-creators with All That Is. I do not wish to be like some scary monster storyteller with this information, but hear me now: the situation on Earth is very, very critical. It becomes more dangerous with each passing day as we create this manuscript. The Laws Of Non-Interference prohibit me from speaking in depth on this matter, the nuclear question, however you must only look at some of your Earth's spiritual traditions, to get an indication of what will inevitably befall you if you continue on your course. The prophecies of these scriptures speak of great fires and catastrophes, and indeed these will occur if humankind does not change its ways. In these same traditions there are writings on how to avoid the cataclysms brought on by greed, ignorance, fear and anger. In a way, my teaching is similar to these ancient - in your terms - manuscripts. I am simply a messenger for All That Is to Westerners in your timeframe.

Please understand that humans at all points of your Earth are being brought up closer to the light in these current years. The people are being educated in their own tongues and with images from their own spiritual and religious teachings.

Atlantis the Technological Power

Atlantis is a society that lingers on the edges of your mass consciousness, almost as a dream. Your people's attraction to the story of Atlantis has to do with the similarities between your cultures. Now without interfering in your evolution, I might say that the similarities revolve around issues of Power with a capital P, the ethical uses of mental technologies and the spirituality question: that is, how does a society protect the open manifestation of spiritual ideas? I trust you may intuit further "talking points" from my humble description.

The greatest technological achievement of the Atlantis civilization - the one that helped create great benefits for the people and advanced the growth of society - was the use of human bioelectric energy in series. The telepathic networks between individuals were used to transmit and magnify human cellular energy. This bioelectric power was then stored in crystals and some special structures made for this purpose. These "batteries" could then power the devices the people used in their daily existences.

Much as modern humans are dependent on electricity from power plants, the Atlanteans required a connection to the storage units that held the energy. This connection was a mental one. The psychic networks that you in your current timeframe are just now beginning to explore and validate, were used in Atlantis in very sophisticated ways. Ordinary human beings could connect to this network mentally and immediately receive the energy transmission, which they would then direct to their devices. I am sorry that I cannot be more forthcoming with this information.

Atlantean Healing

I might add that the people of Atlantis had a unique healing system that utilized color and sound. Prismatic colors and natural as well as "synthesized" sounds and colors, were used by members of the healing caste to effect <u>cures</u> of various diseases. I'm attempting to give Mark an experiential glimpse into these healing practices with a small hologram.

(I closed my eyes and felt the ecstasy Seth describes and I noticed a hum coming from my office computer. It seemed to grow louder in volume and entered my body, cycling up and down from my head to my toes. I felt quite clear-headed and energized afterwards. I got the message that environmental or ambient sounds may be "captured" by one's consciousness and brought into the problem area to heal the body through "resonance." mf)

The healers of Atlantis were actually facilitators of the healing process within individuals. These techniques were similar to your modern hypnosis methods. The subject was led through prescribed visualization journeys to access "the healer within." The power of healing was thought to lie within the Great Power: the Divine or Sacred Energy of Life. Members of the healing caste were in touch with what we are referring to in these writings as the Energy Personality. They were experts in facilitating contact and communication with the Energy Personalities of those they were assisting. The work was very similar to what we are attempting in this current project.

Lemuria

We have covered GA and Atlantis. We will now discuss Lemuria. This civilization is quite active on your planet Earth, yet like others, is flourishing within adjacent dimensions. Now as an intriguing aside to our presentation here Mark, many anomalous phenomena you experience in your timeframe - ghosts, monsters of various types, space beings - are simply your perceptions of momentary openings - portals if you will - into these other dimensions. We will have more to say about this in the Q&A section if you prompt me to answer your specific questions on the matter. *(See the Q&A Section. mf)*

Lemuria the civilization is the stimulus in your human consciousness - collective consciousness - for ideas about underground people. Thus, in your fairy tales you have trolls and other fascinating types of creatures who pop out of the ground to engage in discussions with humans, only to "disappear" back into the Earth. Now it is true, in a sense, that this civilization can be thought of as subterranean, yet that is simply where the Lemurian dimension is located in your Earthly intersection of space and time. To the Lemurians it is you, the surface inhabitants of Earth, who are peculiar in your occupation of the "upper" dimensions of the Lemurian world.

The people of Lemuria are excellent dreamers. They pay much attention to their dream activities and appreciate the connections to the waking physical world. They spend a greater amount of time sleeping than do the inhabitants of your Third-Dimensional world. You often experience their dreams as momentary waking visions, or fantastic dreams if you are asleep. Humans of the Third-Dimension and the subterranean Lemurians share elements of consciousness, therefore, and if you are patient and perceptive, you may identify these bleedthroughs in your own consciousness when they occur.

The underworld people have been the subject of many visitations by shamans and other travelers of the Etheric Realms for centuries on your world. To go into the Earth seeking visions is to invite meetings with these people. Now they have a markedly different appearance than their surface colleagues. I cannot tell you specifics, as I wish you to discover these for yourself. However, I can say that your descriptions of Nature Spirits, the Green Man, Elementals and others are highly accurate. Different physical locations beneath the surface reveal different articulations of the subterranean life forms, just as the different races of humanity are "products" of the different surface conditions on your Earth.

Dear Reader, these descriptions of just a few of your mystery civilizations are necessarily short, however, they will do for our purposes. We are giving you some background to your origins within linear perceptions. In future books, we shall go into much greater detail on these and other aspects of your perceived past.

Dialogue - Bleedthroughs
4/15/04 8:25 am

Mark - *The whole issue of bleedthroughs brings up the question of whether these episodes can also be messages from one's Guides?*

Seth - *They can be. They can also be glimpses of probable roads not taken and so not actualized. For the most part, as I said, in these bleedthrough experiences you are connecting with aspects of your Simultaneous Lives. As I mentioned in Book I,* (Chapter Three. mf) *in the Unity of Consciousness Dimension you will be aware of all of your existences past, present and future and you will be able to remember them and hold those memories. Now, currently your consciousness - and by this I mean the consciousness of Western mankind - is just beginning to learn how to navigate these regions. Part of this learning experience is discovering how to "hold" these perceptive bleedthroughs in your consciousness without resorting to fear, denial, etc. These experiences will be momentary, therefore, until the Inner Senses are adequately developed, and your skills at creating love and confidence out of fear and anger are mastered. You are not given more than you can deal with in any particular instance here. It is an individual learning curve with each of you as you learn to acknowledge your Energy Personalities and begin to expand your perceptions with the help of these Guides. Does this give some clarity to our discussion?*

Mark - *Yes, thanks Seth.*

Experiment - Connecting with Your "Historical" Past
Hypothesis: current interests may illustrate lives in preceding eras

I believe that we have set the stage adequately with our discussion of the origins of humanity as to where you have been in terms of your preceding many thousands of years. This brings us to your present. From this vantage point we can see how each of the readers of this book has participated in these events: being spun off from All That Is and being born as babies and raised in some or all of the great Mystery Civilizations of Earth. Now this leaves us still looking backwards from your present into the ages after these civilizations and leading up to your current incarnations within your modern timeframe.

A very simple way to conduct research into this intermediary phase is to consider, individually Dear Reader, what eras in your Earth's historical past you identify with or feel deeply attached to, as if you had spent some time or even a lifetime in these historical timeframes. This is a potent method of consciousness expansion.

Before you enact your Ritual of Sanctuary, make a list of historical eras you enjoy reading about in books or depicted in motion pictures. Do you feel a sense of nostalgia here? Do you feel a sense of longing, as though you are away from your home? If you do, these eras may merit exploration in this experiment. You may wish to scan some history books for ideas, using your intuition to guide you. When you have your list of eras at hand…

Conduct your Ritual of Sanctuary

Now access your state of relaxation using whatever techniques you have found useful. To repeat the phrase, "I am light," may be helpful. When you are sensing your world in a light and relaxed manner, consider your list of eras one-by-one, and visualize the possibility of your having lived a life within these timeframes. Now often it will appear quite obvious that you are going in the right direction here. You may have a sense of loving acceptance with a re-living of experiences from these possible past existences. Make a mental note to remember this information. When you have finished your list, gently return to your waking consciousness.

Findings - Document your experiences.

Experiment - Daily Forecasting & Projections of Consciousness

Hypothesis: you can prove to yourself that you create your physical reality in the dream state

Try this experiment upon just awakening from sleep in the morning. I specifically say morning, because in the early morning hours one has one foot in the etheric and one foot in the physical. This is the perfect time to witness the manifestation phenomenon.

Conduct your Ritual of Sanctuary

Before sleeping give yourself a suggestion to linger in the state in between sleeping and waking the following morning or whenever you will awaken. Then as you are just coming out of sleep and your suggestion is taking hold, and you are lingering and enjoying it, make a few predictions for yourself on what is going to transpire in your "future" day. Suggest to yourself that you will remember these predictions on fully awakening. When you awaken, write down your forecast for your day. Naturally, the next step would be to go on with your day and notice positive correlations between the items on your forecast and the events in your day. Now, do this for a period of time, as a scientist would, and keep a diary of your experiences. Note here that the correlations denote more than precognitions. They may confirm for you, the waking Soul, that you are experiencing the reality you have just created in the dream state.

With your experiments in forecasting on a daily basis, you will be intimately exposed to the concept of probabilities like never before. The sharpening of the intuition, indeed, is done through an appreciation for the qualities and behavior of probabilities on a personal level in your own life. Probable paths chosen or ignored are the building blocks, so to speak, of your existence. This is a critical point, I think, and so perhaps an example is needed for clarity. Suppose you are at a crossroads of sorts. You are faced with a decision that you must make that will have a great influence on the direction your life will take afterwards. For instance: suppose your job is being moved to another state or another country. Your decision to stay or leave for the distant job site will establish a completely different trajectory of life experiences for you and your family.

Now, with an appreciation of probabilities and some knowledge of the concept of Moment Points and the other ideas we have been discussing in this and my previous book, you can make far better decisions in these matters.

After conducting your Ritual of Sanctuary, you could use a projection of consciousness down the two or three possible trajectories of probability. In a relaxed state, you could visualize the outcome, further down the road, of each probable decision. First, imagine what would occur after a decision to accept the position offered in another state or country. What would the moment-to-moment, day-to-day aftereffects of that decision manifest for you? Fill in the details with emotion and color as best you can. Now mentally return to your current timeframe and imagine the aftereffects, on a day-to-day basis, of your probable decision to stay in your current location, and perhaps find a job with another firm, or perhaps even starting your own business right where you are now. When you sense that your experiment is complete, gently return to fully-awakened consciousness.

Findings - Please document your outcomes the best way that suits you.

Experiment - Connecting with the Mystery Civilizations
Hypothesis: current interests may illustrate lives in the mystery civilizations

Using the methods from a previous experiment, consider which of the Mystery Civilizations you may have resided in. There may have been others not mentioned in this text that you will put on your list. Just get a sense of where your interests have been over the years of your current life. Are you an engineer type or a scientist? Are you a nurturer and yet also a leader? With the knowledge of what type of personality you are currently, consider which of the Mystery Civilizations you may have lived within, that could serve to complement your personality and interests. In past manuscripts I have established for you several families of consciousness. With this in mind - that you may be a participant in a family of consciousness and that you share traits with others in this family - yet without creating unnecessary dogma around it, as I may have done in the past - I would invite you to consider the

49

mystery civilizations that most suit your temperament and personality and put them on your list.

Conduct your Ritual of Sanctuary

As before, create your relaxed state and go through your list. Visualize the possibilities of life within these civilizations. For you it may be as though you are watching a motion picture, or perhaps a particular feeling tone will serve to direct you. The Sumari language is very distinctive, perhaps you will hear some dialogue from a possible existence in GA. As I often tell Mark, "You will know it when you see it or hear it." Watch and listen. Continue this line of inquiry for as long as you wish, without of course, trying to find something that is not there. When you sense that the experiment is over for the time being, gradually come to full-waking consciousness.

Findings - Document your findings.

CHAPTER THREE

The Non-Physical Universe

Dialogue - The Inner Senses
4/14/04 12:33 pm

Mark - Can you speak on the Inner Senses and how we can use them in our experiences?

Seth - Now I can tell by your thoughts that there should be more discussion on the definitions and activities of these Inner Senses. First, the word "inner" may be somewhat confusing, as there is no inner or outer in the true reality of your world, but we use the term to distinguish the Inner Senses from what you call your outer, physical senses. Perhaps "Non-Physical Senses" would be a better term. The answer is, you are already, to a vastly greater degree than most, using your Non-Physical Senses - intuition if you prefer. When you ask a question of me and you "go and get" me, you are using these senses. You are navigating your inner world when you do these activities and in that world you will find different environments, signs and symbols, than

*you will find in your exterior world. Each person is differ-
ent in how they use these Non-Physical Senses and the results they get through these perceptive means are also
unique to the individual. Now this is good, this creative use
of perception, in that All That Is may experience the greatest articulation of emotion, memory, behavior and the like.
Perhaps I am taking the long way around this answer, but
this is simply a prelude to a deeper investigation that we
will embark upon as we create the new material.*

Your Inner World

Everyone has an "inner life," whether they acknowledge
it or not. All of you are involved in the great dramas and
subliminal activities of the underworld of human consciousness. Memories of these experiences are carried out with
you from sleep and you may marvel at the peculiar symbols
of this material. Yet this non-physical universe is ALWAYS
ON, despite your knowing or unknowing of its reality. In
your waking hours, as you go about your work-a-day world
behaviors, this unknown reality of the spirit continues to
unfold beyond your physical senses. Indeed, it is this etheric
counterpart to your physical reality that gives life to your
"normal" waking hours perceptions. The two work together,
in other words - the waking and the sleeping time realities -
to present to you for your edification, the life lessons you
have incarnated to learn.

Now, to get a sense for this complementary non-
physical reality, all you must do is present a line of in-

quiry to yourself, while in a relaxed and open state of mind. This non-physical reality is "waiting in the wings," to enter into your particular life-drama that you are experiencing.

As I have hinted at in these new books, most of you who are reading this material are doing so for a purpose; that is, to catalyze the use of your Inner Senses. In this way, you will be receiving a preview of what is to be humanity's next perceptual breakthrough - an exploration of the Unity of Consciousness Dimension. So your inner world will be making itself known to the outer, in a way never before experienced by humankind. And you have the opportunity of learning about this new land beforehand, so that if you feel called upon to do so, you may assist in the awakening of others. Now let us speak of the creation of the new realities that will bridge the inner to the outer worlds.

Accepted and Rejected Fields of Reality

A critical and necessary aspect of Reality Creation is what we will call the concept of Accepted and Rejected Fields of Reality. Simply put, your beliefs determine what you accept or reject as part of your Personal Reality Field. Another way to express this idea is that each of you, as the creator of your personal world, refer continuously to the thematic structures of your belief system. Moment-to-moment, you accept from innumerable probabilities, those that complement your ongoing Personal Reality Field. You act upon these probabilities and so bring them from the potential and probable into the realm of the possible and actual. Your Personal Reality develops staying power and permanence in this way.

This concept of Accepted and Rejected Fields can be used to explain how your belief system changes as you learn your lessons in Third-Dimensional reality. For example: let us examine a person who may be new to matters spiritual. They are a male or female who has lived a very material life. Their main activities are shopping and watching television. They have not reproduced or built a network of family or friends. This may describe many millions of the inhabitants of your Western world. You could say that their Accepted Field of Reality, the Personal Reality they have known and can come to expect in the future, is one of robotic existence. The inner life is not examined here to any degree. This is simply the way it is for them. But let us suppose that the Higher Self of one of these people creates an opportunity for going within, to perhaps briefly meet the Soul Self. Divine information is streamed into the consciousness of this person. Let us say this has the effect of motivating them to take a walk in the forest rather than spending the day watching television. As this person walks in the forest, they participate in the exchange of energies with the vibrant, life-affirming aspects of the forest environment. This may have the effect of revitalizing and spiritualizing this person, to the degree that they would want to make this activity a regular part of their existence.

Do you see how the chosen activity of walking in the forest, merely one of an infinite number of probable activities, acts to bring new life to this person? Perhaps this is part of their lessons they have come to Earth to learn. Perhaps they are to seek out empowering activities in nature that will expand their consciousness and serve to spin them off onto a different, more life-affirming trajectory than their current life path.

Now, this is of course greatly simplified, this example, for the accepting or rejecting of individual probable actions, ideas and images is infinitely more complex. To bring in the computer analogy here for a moment: the process would be similar to the functioning of the world's most powerful computer. This theoretical computer would be able to make an infinite amount of choices from among an infinite array of probabilities each second. In our previous example, each choice would serve to complement and endorse and continually verify the belief system. And the activity of walking in the forest, done over time, is moving from a Rejected Field of Reality to an Accepted Field of Reality. It is being incorporated into the Personal Reality Field.

Dialogue - Impulses
4/9/04 1:30 pm

Mark - These impulses from our Simultaneous Lives, are they what we would call inspiration or creative thought?

Seth - You are on the right track with this. These impulses are indeed inspirational and creative as you recognize them and use them in the creation of your world. But as we have discussed, many in your world regard these impulses as "voices of the devil," or at the least, untidy remnants of pathology to be suppressed and ignored. To be sure Mark, within this vast chorus of telepathic transmissions, the Negative Entities also vie for attention. But it is a simple matter to protect yourself with your own positive affirmative thoughts when exploring these areas of consciousness. Surrounding yourself with "white light" is a very effective precaution to take before your explorations or meditations. In this way, you focus your attention on the positive and look, you find the positive creative impulses coming into view. This is all simple metaphysics, Mark. You get what you focus on. You create your reality.

Inspiration

Generally, it is quite easy for those of you in the U.S. and some of the other industrialized nations, to think of yourselves as individuals. The pioneer influence is felt by many of you in your cultures and so you fancy yourselves as independent explorers of your personal domains. And so it follows that you feel as though your mental life is your own, and that even though privacy in the personal and business fields of endeavor is rapidly being lost, at least your thoughts are your own, if what you define as "thoughts" are "the greater elements of human mentality."

Yet your thoughts are not truly your own, in this pioneer sense. In the great Gestalt of Consciousness I have been describing to you, the thoughts of your Simultaneous Lives past, present and future are being received by you, as well as the thoughts and suggestions of Beings of Light, the negative transmissions of Nefarious Entities and the telepathic thoughts of your fellow humans.

Your thoughts are alive, Dear Reader. Each of your thoughts, including the thoughtforms transmitted into your consciousness by Energy Bodies and your fellow humans, has a propensity for creating itself in physical reality. And because your human thoughts have distinct properties - such as a "desire" to associate with other similar thoughts, and an energetic ability to transcend space and time - your thoughts can be considered to be the most powerful Energy Constructs in your system of reality.

However, unfortunately for most of you, you begin your lives on Earth by surrendering your powers of thought-creation and manifestation to individuals and institutions. And so you are taught to create with your powerful thoughts, the Reality Constructs of the institutions - family, church, business, country - in which you participate. Many of you abandon your loving, altruistic visions in childhood, therefore, and it may be that you the reader of this book are only now remembering the idealism of your early manifestation activities. These activities may have included collaborations with imaginary playmates. Now I shall discuss this further, this topic of childhood Spirit

57

Guides, in future volumes. For now simply note that there are a host of potential relationships with "imaginal" beings available to you within the sphere of your personal consciousness.

Special Impulses

In my first book since my return to publishing, I provided an illustration for you on how to send out energy - positive, loving energy - to your Simultaneous Lives. In the experiment at the end of this chapter, you will be "completing the circuit" by discerning with your awareness, when the responses in the form of special impulses, are entering your consciousness. This is not hard to do. As I have just mentioned, in each and every day of your existence on Earth, you have a multitude of impulses entering your awareness, each vying for your attention. These impulses, however, the special impulses I am now discussing, are easily recognizable for what they are, by virtue of their obvious loving utility.

When one of these impulses is recognized, you have an immediate sense of rightness, as though you wonder why it took so long for the idea to come around. These ideas are also based in a truly loving aspect of consciousness that is undeniable. In essence, this loving energy is the energy of All That Is transmitted through your various Simultaneous Lives, and then captured by you as your consciousness participates in the Gestalt of Awareness that IS you and your many lives past, present and future. These impulses may be accompanied by synchronous events and a sense of wonder and divine bemusement. Everything comes together in your life drama for the benefit of your learning experience. These synchronicities and thus the life lessons may be brought into your awareness intentionally. Look to the experiments at the end of this chapter for further information

So you the reader, when engaged in this dialogue with your Simultaneous Lives, are receiving the benefits of learning experience from the personalities who are LIVING these many lives. In fact, just as I Seth am now returning to my past through my human counterparts to educate and inform humanity on the very, very serious issue of the survival of the species- and for that matter the planet Earth - these communiqués from your Simultaneous Lives in the form of impulses serve to educate and inform you the reader, on a personal level with regards to appropriate action you can take to improve your life. I would like to restate my point regarding these types of messages and all messages from your Higher Self: these messages are benign and loving in their intent and that is how you can tell they are from your Higher Self. And as always, free will is operative; you can choose to act on or ignore these impulses.

Your Simultaneous Lives

This illustration may serve as a graphic example of how you and your Simultaneous Lives are engaged in this continuous exchange of impulses and energy I am describing. As you can see, you are at the heart of this reciprocal activity. You occupy the center in your Gestalt of Consciousness: the energy network that comprises the receiving and sending of impulse energies between your current self and all of your other selves past, present and future. This very basic activity of consciousness rests within a framework that is totally dependent on the loving and creative energies of All That Is. And the culmination of all of these energies within your individual consciousness at any one moment, can be described as "the activity of the conscious mind." Should you wish to consider these ideas while using the illustration as a meditation focus piece, you may perceive for yourself more intimate meanings than any of my explanations can provide.

Mark's Ancestor

Now as an example here on how impulses may be experienced within your life, let us discuss the case of Mark's ancestor. Several years ago he conducted some research into the life of a man from his mother's side of the family and he vicariously lived some of the exciting episodes of this man's life as he transcribed the biographical narrative into his computer. I can tell you that there was more to it than simply imagining himself in the time period and ac-

IMPULSES AND SIMULTANEOUS LIVES

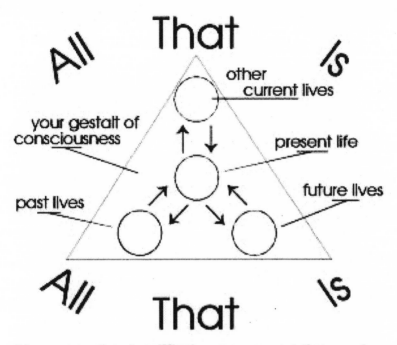

That

All

Is

your gestalt of
consciousness

other
current lives

present life

past lives

future lives

All

That

Is

Now, greatly simplified... you are at the center
of your Gestalt of Consciousness in your current
Moment Point in your Present Life. You send
out energy to your Past, Present and Future
lives. These lives receive the transmissions as
impulses just as you receive impulses from
your Simultaneous Lives Past, Present and
Future. You and your Simultaneous Lives use
your free will to either act upon or ignore these
impulses. This interplay of sending and receiving
impulses accounts for much of what you would
call "the activity of the conscious mind."

~ Seth

tivities of this ancestor. Mark had a direct connection to this fellow, though not in an ancestral lineage, for as I have stated before, these sequential networks of relations do not necessarily exist physically.

(I did transcribe from notes into my computer, biographical events from the life of a relative of mine. I wanted to preserve these writings of my relative's great great-granddaughter and I did make copies of the work and gave them to various members of my family. Briefly, a man on my mother's side of the family led a Mormon battalion from the Eastern U.S. to Utah, where they settled in their "Promised Land." He led an exciting life and died of a serious injury to his arm. Recently I have come to understand the similarities between my ancestor leading his people to the Promised Land and Seth and I leading people into the Fourth Dimension. I have also entertained the notion that perhaps my ancestor may have felt that he was communicating with an Angel or other spirit when he was contacting me from the past. mf)

For now, let us explore this relationship of Mark with his male ancestor. In past writings, I have described the true nature of human relationships over the generations. Your lives are essentially simultaneous, and those of you reading this book, in this moment, are experiencing this particular Moment Point in one of your Simultaneous Lives. This Dear Reader, is simply one Point of Power in literally millions and millions of probable and chosen Points of Power in which you are participating. So let us suppose for a moment that Mark, even as he participates in his current Point of Power - he is taking dictation from me - he also is participating in countless other Points of Power within his numerous Simultaneous Lives past, present and future. So do you see that when Mark vicariously enjoyed the adventures of his noted male ancestor several years ago, he was also, at that Moment Point, quite literally experiencing his ancestor's reality from within his ancestor's Moment Point. In other words, he was sharing his ancestor's Point of Power experiences as he was working with the written material, organizing it on his computer and so on. This is a literal fact. Astounding as it may be to some readers, this type of thing goes on continuously in your own private lives. You "leave the body," to coin one of your phrases, and travel inter-dimensionally to participate in these activities. Often you can do so while carrying on a conversation with one of your fellow humans and appear quite normal. Your eyes may glaze over a bit; an indication that you are traveling and experiencing other timeframes.

Now, your scientists may characterize this as pathological, dissociation, fantasy, escape; completely missing the importance of what is occurring. I don't want to go off on one of my critiques here, but let me say this: until your scientists can learn to turn their empirical noses inwardly, they will not be able to sniff out one iota of truth regarding human consciousness, or the human condition or the human Soul.

Gentle Persistence

I would like to emphasize that in these matters of Soul exploration, you can be quite successful with a gentle, yet persistent effort. Your initial experiments in accessing your Inner Senses are an exercise in subtlety. Approach these activities with an eye on gradual results over time. The clouds, in most instances, do not part and reveal the Etheric Visions to you, after only a few attempts in your experiments in the field.

I realize that this subtle route to discovery may be difficult for those of you who have expectations of immediate results. Some of you may be of the mind that, like everything else in your Western world of mass-consumption, if it is not forthcoming immediately, on your schedule, because you have so much "to do," that it may not be worth attempting. To these readers I say, take the time necessary to accomplish your goals in this Soul Work. One of your sayings extols the virtues of waiting with patience for the truly beneficial aspects of your life to materialize. And honestly, the days of instantaneous manifestation are still in your perceived future. These experiments will give you an advantage for the time when you will be experienced enough to use your Inner Senses appropriately for the instantaneous manifestation of Reality Constructs.

Now once again I would remind you that all of these experiments are designed to lead to the uncovering and practical use of your Inner Senses. And these Inner Senses are what you may broadly term "intuition." In past writings I have lectured on how the intuition can be divided into separate senses and I did indeed name them. I sense (humorously) that it may have been a mistake to do so, for it is now several decades later and I am still waiting for my many readers to make practical use of that material. For now we will simplify this labeling and refer to the phenomenon as the use of the Inner Senses and allow each reader to do whatever delineation they may, as they discover the attributes of these senses for themselves - again, learning by doing, and perhaps creating their own names for their experiences.

Dialogue - Witchcraft
4/4/04 45 pm

Mark - Can you speak about my difficulties with concepts such as Astral Travel, Soul Work and other esoteric ideas?
Seth - The experience of Astral Travel, as some have called it, is quite common among you. It is a refreshing experience, after having say, engaged in a difficult day at your job, to simply cast off from the physical, as I said, even while engaged in other activities with your fellow humans, and travel the subtle levels. Now Mark, I know that you find the term Astral Travel a bit distasteful, perhaps because you associate it with images of quacks, charlatans etc. etc. etc. You have your fears that you may be branded a charlatan, for indeed in several of your simultaneous existences, you were accused and punished for practicing witchcraft. These lives took place in different historical eras,

I should mention. So you have a built in prejudice here. This is not necessarily for the book, but could be if you are willing to open up. Am I understood?
Mark - *Yes, Seth, you are understood. I don't mind using this material for the book. I do think I am opening up to my multi-dimensional being. What do you think?*
Seth - *Mark, you are doing quite well, and I give you excellent "marks" in those endeavors (humorously). Now, to continue... If you choose to use this for the book this will make a fine segue...*

Intention

So Dear Reader, witness how our friend Mark is opening up to his greater reality simply by affirming it. That is how you do it: with your thoughts, just like everything else in your reality. Have the intention that you are opening up to these Simultaneous Lives of which we are speaking, and soon enough, proof of their reality will be presented to you. Now, without belaboring the example of Mark and his illustrious ancestor, it was on IMPULSE that he decided to transcribe the material into a more readable format. His intuitive voice spoke to him and promised him that much of value and interest could be recovered if he were to do so. So where did the voice come from? In Mark's case it was from his ancestor personally, though this is by no means the rule in these phenomena. His ancestor reached across the timeframes into his future, to communicate with Mark and motivate him. Now this may sound fantastic to some of you. Indeed it will remain unbeliev-able and so un-witnessed by you in your own realities. The following experiments may help you prove to your-selves that you are ALREADY active participants in the non-physical reality.

Experiment - Discovering the Inner Senses
Hypothesis: the intuitive senses may be strengthened through use.

And so what are these Inner Senses? Briefly, they are both the creators and the perceiving apparatus of your world. In your Third-Dimensional existence, you create out of Consciousness Units your physi-cal realities, and then instantaneously perceive your creations as a form of feedback of this endeavor, the creation of worlds. In past manuscripts I have often informed you of your god status. It is difficult for you humans to take seriously this talk of godlike abilities, for many of you have been indoctrinated by your various religions to be meek, to be mild, to obey. And as I have stated in my previous book, after transferring your power to your religions, you then transferred your power to your governing insti-tutions and to your scientists. What I propose to you here in this book is that you are not meek, mild and obedient unless you truly wish to be so. You are whoever you THINK you are and you have the power in this moment to completely change who you are. That is because YOU are at the center of your world as the ultimate creative force. With the energy of All That Is, you as co-creator do indeed manifest from your beliefs and ideas of what is possible, your perceived reality.

Now, without further lecturing (humorously), we will give a short description of the experiment. It builds upon a simpler one described in my earlier book in which I asked the reader to get a sense of the wonder of their own Personal Reality. Here we will take it further. We will be taking the senses back into the inner world. As I suggested in the first chapter, the physical senses grew out of the Inner Senses, of necessity, to perceive the exterior, physical Universe. The Inner Senses from which these outer, physical senses were derived, are awaiting your discovery and use within your mental environment.

Perform Your Ritual of Sanctuary.

You have several physical senses: sight, hearing, taste, touch and smell. Your Inner Senses are complementary to these outer senses, yet they go beyond the physical senses in capabilities. For example: let us get a feel for the Inner Sense that may be a complement to the outer sense of sight. You may relax a bit for this experiment, yet you needn't close your eyes. We will be relying on your sense of physical sight to conduct this experiment. With the eyes open, yet with

the relaxation and contentment that comes with the state of Sanctuary you are embodying, can you see the deeper, perhaps symbolic meanings entailed in your Personal Reality Field? Remember here: everything in your field of perception is a reflection of an interior reality. As you consider this statement, you may find that your visual field begins to swirl a bit, as the etheric blends with the exterior. Go with this flow of blending transformation for a few moments until you have observed noteworthy findings. Gradually come back to your physically-perceived world. Naturally you may experiment further with the complements to the other senses to gain more information.
Findings - Document your findings.

Experiment - Recognizing Special Impulses
Hypothesis: some thoughts are special impulses from your simultaneous lives

This experiment is one that you can do on an ongoing basis as you go about your life, doing those things that you normally do, engaged in the mundane experiences of your existence. Some of you may have noticed that much of this life is lived in a rote fashion, by habit, almost as if in a dream. Then something occurs in your consciousness to pull you out of the habitual pattern. A sudden thought might occur to you the reader, that you can easily change your course somewhat and experience a new avenue of exploration in your life. Now this impulse might be quite simple, as simple as changing the type of breakfast cereal you eat. Or this fleeting idea might urge you to consider breaking off a relationship that has been negative for some time. Often these ideas can present new opportunities to your awareness, so that in retrospect, perhaps after several months or years, you realize that your acting on the impulse had the effect of completely transforming your life. You are amazed at how the alternate path taken had set up a series of alternate events that led to a uniquely different, and often more positive and life-affirming outcome, than had you continued on your habitual path of experience. It is these special impulses we will be exploring in this experiment. These may indeed be impulses from your Simultaneous Lives, offering you suggestions for creating more productive Reality Constructs in your life.

Conduct your Ritual of Sanctuary

Now use your relaxation techniques to create a relaxed state within your body. There are two approaches to recognizing special impulses: First, you may work your way back in time from the present regarding a special impulse that you noticed and acted upon which spun you off into a new, positive direction. You can then see the context of influences you were in that created this catalyst for action. Then recreate this context in your present moment - emotional content, physical circumstances - through use of the imagination. Consider these special impulses within your consciousness NOW that may be these messages from other parts of yourself. Write them down. Act on them if appropriate using you free will. Second, if you cannot think of a special impulse you have acted upon, simply relax into your meditation and ask for the special impulses to present themselves to your awareness. Then write them down and either act on them or not. This practice leads to experiences of synchronicity, wonder, amusement and awe. **Findings** - Document your findings rigorously.

Experiment - Cultivating Synchronicity
Hypothesis: you may anticipate, create and sustain coincidental events within your personal reality field

In this experiment you will attempt to intentionally create coincidental events within your Personal Reality Field. This experiment is most easily conducted when you are experiencing the coincidental events in your current Moment Point. As you gain experience in observing your consciousness and the synchronous events you participate in, it will become easier to anticipate coincidental events. You will be able to sense them coming to you from the future. Now you are creating these future events from your current moment, you see. As you are experiencing the wonder, awe and amusement that comes with this type of experience, you will be pleasantly motivated to continue with your research. Remember that you may use your powers of intent to extend these feelings and these events for some time.

Conduct Your Ritual of Sanctuary

Pick out anything in your field of perception. For example: say to yourself that the bird in the tree in front of you will now be a part of a coincidental event with something else in your Personal Reality Field. Quite soon after this inner declaration, watch your environment closely for the coincidental experience. You are using your imagination to create a synchronous event, you see, that will then be fabricated out of CUs for your viewing within your Personal Reality. You may then "expect" a third synchronous event to materialize, and so on. This is very much like child's play, and is quite a fun way to spend a few minutes of your day.

Findings - Document your findings.

CHAPTER FOUR

Contacting the Energy Personality

Dialogue - Proof
6/17/04 9:30 am

Mark - *Seth, can you give me some physical proof that what you say to me is true?*

Seth - *Graphic examples, Mark, proof is all around you. Now, just minutes ago you asked for information from an associate who was unconscious and you received it from them.* (This person was in a coma. mf) *These types of communications will be commonplace in just a few years in your reality. This will be so, partly, because we will be educating the public on how to develop these communications. Again, the closer you look at your perceived reality - the Personal Reality Field that you co-create with All That Is according to your beliefs - the more validation you receive for what I have been saying to mankind for decades in these writings. Each moment of perceived reality serves as a graphic example of the manifestation of thought into physicality that is at the heart of my many messages to you in the Third Dimension. There is the proof my friend. You construct your physical reality from the blueprints of your beliefs.*

The Energy Personality

The Energy Personality, which is related to the Soul, will be the etheric teacher to those of you who are to experience the transition into the Unity of Consciousness Dimension with your "eyes wide open." You will have read my new books or received messages from me or other Energy Personalities and you will have acted on the advice given you. Many of you, without recognizing the fact, have already been given instruction on the use of your Inner Senses, what to expect in the Fourth Dimension, how to move beyond fear and anger and into love and confidence and other subjects of great importance. In the dream state you are being "brought up to speed" by those of us who teach on the subtle levels. And so now you are reading this book and perhaps having a singular sense of familiarity, déjà vu, as though you have done this before, with accompanying feelings of pleasure, "elementary ecstasy" as my friend Mark describes it. Your world is larger and more complex than you know - your world meaning your created reality. You have physical teachers and you have "metaphysical" teachers, all of you, and now it is time to introduce you to the metaphysical Guides who have been with you since your birth into your dimension.

74

When you ask for your Energy Personality to come forth into your awareness, you may feel that sense of familiarity. For even though you have been pretending that ghosts do not exist ever since your childhood ended - adults do not have imaginary friends, after all - on a deeper level you will recognize these connections. Now you may not be willing to admit these relationships to the world because of fear of being exposed. However, and to illustrate my point, currently a cycle in human consciousness is coming to an end and a new cycle is beginning. You are gradually becoming aware of your connections to your Guides, your Simultaneous Lives, and other energy forms within your Gestalt of Awareness. You need only look at the headlines in your daily newspapers to notice how many changes are upon you in your Third-Dimensional reality. With the ending of an era comes dramatic change amid much clinging, by some, to outmoded belief systems. Yet know this: the more you cling to the past, the more likely you will be relegated to the past when the transition is complete. The new world for humanity is being created in the dream state by all of you as you participate in the manifestation of your collective consciousness.

In your dream state, you freely collaborate with your Energy Personality and other Guides in the creation of incipient Reality Constructs that are manifested on awakening. This is how you create your reality with All That Is. Naturally, this phenomenon is much more complicated than I have described, but that does not mean that you cannot grasp it experientially. Please see the experiments at the end of this chapter.

Encouragement and Caution

As I have said earlier, your human consciousness visits other time periods and participates in activities in other dimensions, even as you may be participating in your daily unremarkable activities. You are experts at vacating your human bodies and venturing forth into the unknown realities. Your New Age metaphysical literature is quite filled with stories of angels, demons, extra-terrestrials and the like. So too do your motion picture businesses prosper through the creation of science fiction and fantasy movies. Yet does it surprise you that these stories are "literally" true? Remember, Dear Reader, that it is your human consciousness that creates your reality in tandem with All That Is. And so the creativity of your artists, as well as your own, feeds and supports alternate dimensions. When you are experiencing these tales, either through reading books or watching movies or plays, you are submerged in the alternate dimensions for that time. So this is the simplest example of inter-dimensional travel - experiencing entertainment media.

With regards to the subject of contacting other Entities in the Fourth Dimension, I must caution you to certainly create your Ritual of Sanctuary and have this ritual memorized. As an explorer of these realms, you undoubtedly will encounter negative energy forms that may come into your consciousness and attempt to fix on your light. By this I mean these Negative Entities can transmit a propensity for negative, repetitive thoughts or images entering your consciousness that can be difficult to undo. You recognize these circular ideas or information loops as disturbing pangs of dread, and other negative emotions. They seem to come from nowhere. Actually these negative energies are attracted to specific memories and ideas you are holding in your mental environment that are of a negative nature: ideas and feelings of low self-worth, replays of past mistakes and all of the other negative inner experiences humans punish themselves with every day.

Now this is how the Negative Forces gain control over the minds of many in your world. They gain a stronghold in a sense, within the mental environment of those with weakened protection systems. It is as though the immune system of the Etheric Body is weakened through the activity of the negative thoughts, images and such, creating the conditions within the mental environment for viral contamination. The negative, circular thoughts - the thought viruses - are then free to multiply. The comparison is very useful here. With our suggestions and experiments we are using love and acceptance and confidence to dispel the viral attack. To carry it further, antibodies are created with the introduction of positive thoughts and emotions into the suppressed immune system of the Mental or Etheric Body. The negative viral front is neutralized and overcome by love, acceptance and confidence. To be sure, a healthy mental, emotional and spiritual body is one that is nourished on love, acceptance and confidence, to the degree that these positive states of consciousness are the typical experiences of the embodied Soul.

Making Contact

Now, I trust that our valued reader has discovered that what we are indeed offering in this book are the steps you can take to contact and communicate with those such as myself: Beings of Light. I am a Light Body of pure energy, that is, information, and I have dedicated myself to service to mankind, just as others, your Guides, have dedicated themselves to serving you. Now some of you may ask, "Is there a chance that I can tune-in to Seth?" The answer is, only if you are a part of The Seth Entity and only if many precise criteria are met.

As I have mentioned before, The Seth Entity in its vastness, communicates with countless Souls in your reality and in other dimensions. Some of these receivers know that they are being spoken to and develop a dialogue and others do not; they simply believe they are inspired. My advice is to not worry about who you are contacting, as long as you are receiving the loving aspect. The open-heart aspect of the communication denotes that you have made contact with the Energy Personality. You will know this feeling, in that it is love embodied. Love as an idea or an ideal is a mental construct. The ecstasy I am describing is felt throughout the body. There is a sense of being pressed in by love so that you have a feeling of slight discomfort mixed in with the pleasurable emotion of love. You will know it when you feel it. It can be experienced as a wave of pleasant emotion, as I describe it to Mark sometimes. Yet each of you will experience it in a different way. This is your Soul shining through. This is the experience of dropping the ego and allowing your Soul Self to perceive your world.

Now, you are on a path of development. All of you are at various stages of Soul Evolution. The difference becomes whether you acknowledge to yourself that you are ready to work with your Energy Personality and move FORWARD in your development. By doing so, you catalyze the great powers within and without. You focus your intent and with the assistance of All That Is, you take a divergent path; a path that will take you from sleep into awakening in a Soul sense. New positive probable futures arise from this intentional choice you make to co-create with All That Is a spiritually-informed existence.

Dialogue - Learning to Communicate
3/29/04 8:53 pm

Mark - Do you want to comment on how I'm doing as a channel of your messages?
Seth - Yes Mark. Now you are just beginning to get it. My books are collections, really, collections of these little essays that we have created. You need not feel as

though you have to come up with a certain amount of pages per session. In the beginning, we will be satisfied with what we get, will we not?

Mark - *OK*

Seth - *You are just learning to pick up the thread. Now there is much to learn on my part also as I somewhat struggle to create this material in sequence, in the same sequence that it will appear in the printed book. If I fail Mark, please forgive me. We will certainly be able to come back at it and create transitions, chapter headings and such, to make the material flow. We will create a nice Seth book for the readers while you will be learning to channel my messages.*

Picking Up the Thread

"Picking up the thread" is a statement I use with my Third Subject to describe the activity of connecting in a relaxed way to my communication stream. It is a subtle endeavor to trust that the material one is writing down or speaking is from The Seth Entity. It is as subtle as picking up a thread from a tapestry of a greater work, to coin a phrase for the reader. The activity of asking for the name of the Energy Personality and having received the name, continuing to seek a mental dialogue with the Energy Personality, is a delicate endeavor. The usual approach is one of hopeful, trusting questioning, done on a regular basis, that leads to two-way telepathic conversations. The questioner asks for the name and receives the name. The questioner asks questions and the answers begin to flow from the source, the Higher Self of the questioner. It is a simple task that you must do diligently and with the proper positive attitude to get results over time.

Mark is experiencing this phenomenon at this moment in our communications. He becomes somewhat drowsy and yawns often, which helps him relax into the feeling. He closes his eyes to focus on the experience of contact. When he feels that I have integrated my energies with his so that work can be done, he opens his eyes and I begin to transmit my information to his apparatus. Often he will look at his hands, thinking they are rather strange looking. This is myself looking through his eyes. These matters of personal contact and communication develop in individual ways, according to peculiarities of personality, the mental environment and the energy within the subject's Reality Field.

As I have stated in previous manuscripts, I must fine-tune my energies to a particular wavelength to make these connections. In this instance, Mark also fine-tunes his energies to meet me in "that space in between worlds" as he is so fond of saying. But just take it as an interesting game. "Don't stress," to coin a phrase. In fact, trying too hard can subvert the process. Diligence with ease is the way to go.

Signs of Integration

The signs of integration are common to all who undertake these explorations in human consciousness. For that reason, I will now spend more book time documenting these effects. I will read the effects Mark is experiencing, through his apparatus at this time. Now you can go deeper. Just close your eyes and intend to deepen this connection.

(I did as Seth suggested. mf)

There is a marked heaviness one feels throughout the body, but especially the head and chest, when one is in contact with the Energy Personality. Mark experiences it as a pleasant "pressing in" on his body from without. It is as if the air pressure of the atmosphere is increased somewhat and one is invited to slow down one's physical and mental activities and focus within. Of course, different personalities may experience different sensations. These are simply the broader physical effects experienced by most people. The emotional element is striking, I think, in that one feels one's self supported on a pleasant wave of good feelings. This is the ecstasy that comes with contact.

Now, knowing what to expect, you can set yourself up for the experience itself. By this I mean, you can cultivate this sense of riding a wave of ecstatic emotion just below the surface of consciousness; and this sense of being comfortably pressed in by the environment that surrounds you; and a sense that you are supported like a beloved child. One embodies these emotions and sensings as a means to prepare the mental and physical environments for contact with the Higher Self, the Energy Personality. Having achieved these conditions, it would be a simple matter to ask for the name of your Guide, perhaps asking for the one "closest" to you to come forward and make contact, for one has many Guides. One must be selective at first.

So you have prepared the emotional and physical space for contacting and communicating with your Energy Personality. Next you can increase the odds of making contact by "invoking" an attitude or a sense of "hopeful, faithful expectation." Here you are anticipating in a positive, loving way, the contact - the encounter. Now as I said, over time you will make contact and succeed in connecting with your Energy Personality whenever you wish. Some will succeed sooner and some later in these experiments. It is important to keep a positive expectation during these attempts and to keep negativity at bay.

Dialogue - Seth Leads Mark into Trance
4/9/04 9:23 am

Mark - *How can I tell if you are completely "in place" before I begin sessions with you?*
Seth - *Mark, this is a mental overshadowing and so you will not get the types of experiences my Second Subject told you about while creating Book I. For you I am developing intense and meaningful transmissions without the sometimes, uncomfortable feelings associated with the fully physical overshadowing. Now you have a fine mind and you can hold the transmission quite steadily. You needn't worry about the quality of the transmission or whether it is "just as effective" as others. This is our new collaboration Mark. It is*

unfolding quite well and you should be pleased with your-self at coming so far in such a short time.

Now, it is possible for you to fine tune this trance of ours simply by intending to do so, relaxing, making one of your restful sounds and easing into the deeper, for want of a bet-ter word, "realms."

(I did as he instructed. mf}

Seth - *There, now you did feel, did you not, that wave of ecstasy just below the surface?*

Mark - *Yes, I did.*

Seth - *There is where you want to be for these transmis-sions Mark. This feeling of pleasure is what can motivate you and our fellow Scientists of Consciousness. You are sigh-ing now and that is appropriate. Now take it further a bit and then we will begin...*

If You Already Know Your Guides

For those of you who are already in communication with your Guides, this book can serve as a means for further explorations. You can access the constellation of Guides you have watching over you. It is possible for any one human, with determination and insight, to culti-vate communications with many Beings of Light. The only limitations to these explorations are the ones you put on them. Documenting your explorations in the fin-est detail seems to be imperative for these voyages within: asking for the names of the various entities, feeling them out for what services they offer, keeping everything organized in the physical arena, and so on. Now let us proceed with some experimentation.

Experiment - Contacting the Energy Personality
Hypothesis: your spirit guide is awaiting contact

In my last book, I included some powerful exercises for engaging your Soul Self. This current experiment can be thought of as building on those exercises, so that you will become proficient as you go along, practicing in sequence as much as you can.

Conduct Your Ritual of Sanctuary

I would like you the reader, just for a few moments, to relax and to close your eyes. Now Mark is the hypnotist, but those of you who have read my earlier works know that I am also quite skilled in these matters. I use these techniques to create the right energy environment for these sessions. This is easy to do. Quiet your mind. Think of a relaxing scene. Now imagine that you have contact with that part of you that is all-knowing - for indeed you do. Ask for its name. Some have referred to these entities as Spirit Guides and this is a good description. Ask it for its name and you will receive it. It may take a few moments to achieve contact. It may take a few more minutes for the name of your Guide to come to you. Be patient. The important thing is to have the expectation that you will achieve contact. And working from the loving aspect of consciousness always, this will keep you moving in the right direction. When you receive the name of your Energy Personality, you may sense that you are re-kindling a past relationship, possibly dating back to your childhood or even beyond that into what you may term "past lives." This remembrance, along with the loving aspect, is a firm indication that you are indeed engaging your Spirit Guide. The excitement that comes with contact may throw you out of trance. Simply try it again after performing the Ritual of Sanctuary. This experiment can be done on a daily basis to strengthen the connection to your Energy Personality. **Findings** - Immediately document your findings.

Experiment - Techniques for Collaboration.
Hypothesis: the energy personality is the genie of literature

Conduct Your Ritual of Sanctuary

A very helpful technique is to ask your Energy Per-sonality to remind you when you are lapsing into self-abusive, negative thoughts or behaviors. Simply present this idea while you are in communication with your Energy Personality. You can decide on what-ever agreed-upon symbol, thought or feeling will rep-resent the communication from the Energy Person-ality that you are veering off of your thought-path. It is indeed a wake-up call from your Higher Self. Now, you use your free will to decide to listen to the warning or ignore it. And again, if the communication is delivered within a loving context of thought and emotion, you can be quite certain it is from the Energy Personality.

You may wish to have your Energy Personality with you at all times, "on-call," to consult at any moment you wish throughout the day. Simply make that arrangement with your Energy Personality. You will find that they are often amenable to your suggestions. Indeed, they are there to carry out your suggestions, without of course, interfering with the evolution of your Soul. The "Genie in the bottle" may come to mind and other mythological descriptions from writers and artists of the past. No, this is not a new phenomenon. The Energy Personality has been in existence from the beginning of your human consciousness. What IS new, is that in these writings we are describing the methods for calling the Energy Personality forward, in a book that will be distributed throughout the world and used by hopefully many thousands of people to help in their Soul's evolution.

Experiment - The Energy Personality as Self-Observer
Hypothesis: your energy personality can monitor your conscious state and give you valuable feedback

You are gods studying your manifestations. I make this statement once again, reminding you of your status as creators of worlds. As humans, you are endowed with the virtually unlimited powers of creation to manifest your desires into physical constructs. This happens <u>naturally</u>, all by itself. It may be somewhat difficult to study this manifestation phenomenon, for you yourself are part of your creation. Therefore, in this experiment, you may attempt to inhabit an alternate perspective in order to study this creation activity you do in tandem with All That Is. It is somewhat like taking snapshots of moments in linear time - the perceptual illusion - for consideration at a "later" date. Let us label this aspect of the Energy Personality the "Self Observer." This aspect of consciousness has the power to "recall" elapsed Moment Points for purposes of inquiry into the nature of events in physical reality. This observing self has the attributes that you endow it with by virtue of your god-like powers of creativity.

The purpose of this experiment is to have your Energy Personality witness and "document" for you, notable excursions into the unknown reality while you are awake. Your Energy Personality will recall instances of Astral Travel, communications with Simultaneous Lives, and other phenomena for review at a later date. This is your Self Observer aspect that you may use to remind you of what you have experienced throughout any given day.

Conduct Your Ritual of Sanctuary

Now create your relaxed mental and physical environment. Then simply assign the task of self-observation to your Energy Personality, much as you would assign a task to a personal assistant. For example: you might say, "Please document as memories today, my voyages into other dimensions, for review this evening." Then mark out time in the evening for review. At that time, ask your Energy Personality to release those memories into your consciousness sequentially for your review. Now obviously you may have your review at other parts of the day or immediately after the notable event. This protocol is simply one of convenience for those of you who have busy daytime working lives.

As you continue with your regimen of self-observation, you may notice that inter-dimensional travel is the rule rather than the exception. You are subject to frequent "mental vacations" of this type throughout your waking and especially your sleeping times. In fact, the great majority of your day-to-day life is spent within these alternate dimensions.

Findings - Document your findings with successfully eliciting information from your Energy Personality on events which have transpired.

CHAPTER FIVE

The Magical Perspective

Dialogue - Visualizing Specifics
3/23/04 4:29 pm

Mark - Continuing our discussion regarding my house and land... some traditions state that you don't have to visualize the specifics of how you will get what you ask for in the manifestation. Is there truth there - that you allow the Universe to fill in the specifics?

Seth - Mark, it is the same answer as before. You create your reality out of Consciousness Units down to the most minute detail. You do this, for the most part, unconsciously. My advice would be for you to be as specific as you possibly can - consciously. "The great, untapped powers of the human mind," as you are so fond of saying, will do the rest. But these natural forces must be given direction, most assuredly. So you need not be superstitious regarding how much "energy" you give a project. You need not feel afraid of "visualizing" too much or asking for too much. Yet your creations are created in complete unison and agreement with your beliefs and your ideas about what is possible. So if you can indeed maintain this magical perspective we have been discussing, moment-to-moment, appreciating the Universe as reflexive, responsive to your every whim, you will in all likelihood get excellent results in a short amount of time.

The Great Work

In your esoteric literature there is much talk of the Perfected Human and the best means to achieve that state of development. Here in this current work, we are exploring similar territory with regards to the transformation of the "baser" human aspects - anger, fear, hatred - into their divine counterparts - love, understanding and courage. In many ways, my teaching has been a continuation of these esoteric studies and philosophies initiated by humans in your perceived past. I must add, that these humans were in close touch with their Energy Personalities and other Guides, as they created these great works of "inspired" literature. It seems obvious to me given what I have described for you in my recent communications, but the whole of inspired literature is infused with the divine information imparted to human authors by Light Bodies such as myself.

Inspired ideas are, for the most part, just that - inspiration or spirit ideation or communication. Quite literally, your Guides, acknowledged as such or not, are responsible for most of the "spirited," life-affirming ideas you have ever entertained or acted upon. Now this may seem to refute my other statements that the impulses conveyed by your Simultaneous Lives are what make up the great percentage of what you would call "the activity of the conscious mind." This remains true. Beings of Light within this milieu of a collective consciousness, seed your mentality with inspired and beneficial ideas, images and feelings. There is no contradiction when you consider the vastness of human consciousness: the webwork of Simultaneous Lives contributing thoughtforms, your own individual Personal Reality consciousness and the lattice of Light Body communication that supports and nourishes it all upon a foundation of limitless creative energy that is All That Is.

Now such profound pronouncements may have the potential of leaving you feeling somewhat diminished. I would remind you then, that YOU are creating this Personal Reality Field of yours, in tandem with All That Is. You are the magician. You are the creative ally with the Divine who creates your part of the world, and as a member of the collective of humans, the world consensus reality.

And this brings up another salient point… many of you have NOT been listening to the voices of the Divine. Many of you have turned a deaf ear to the suggestions of Beings of Light. That is why you find yourselves in such dire circumstances. So there is a balance, Dear Reader, that you can achieve here. The perfected human is one who balances the inputs of divine information with their own Reality Creation agendas, within the greater dramas of learning one's lessons. Perhaps "perfected" is not quite the right word. "Adequate" may be a better term. For adequate is all one must be to begin and continue the Great Work - the learning of lessons on the path of Soul Evolution. The concept of a humble god may also serve us well here. You are gods who have all power, but without the HUMILITY gained from lessons learned, you do not serve your world in beneficial ways. Obviously many of you are contributing to the critical state of affairs on your planet. You may be required to return again to the material plane until you have learned this greatest of lessons.

The Magical Perspective

The topic for discussion is the magical perspective. I gave my First Subject and her husband a great deal of material on this topic. They assembled it into a book and published it. I am sure that it was purchased by many people and read by them. However, I am just as certain that few of these readers took the time to absorb the meaning and consider the potential inherent in the ideas presented in that book. I am just as certain that the great majority of readers of my past works created so long ago, did not take the time to work with the material to the extent that they received the ultimate benefits possible from doing so. I do not mean to chastise my devoted readers, however I must bring up a salient point here: if the many readers of the old material had indeed taken the ideas to heart and created for themselves the loving Reality Constructs based on the virtues of humankind, there would be no need for me to return and write these new books through my human counterparts. This should be obvious to most of you, why I have returned.

Now in particular, the book *The Magical Approach*, like my early work *Seth Speaks*, presented some very powerful means for altering the reader's Personal Reality in beneficial ways. The new volumes I am creating here in the new millennium with my Second and Third Subjects have that same potential. Yet potential will remain just that if it is not acted upon. A probability of altered realities for the better will remain a probability if not acted upon. Again this should be obvious to all of you, but it is the acting upon the impulse, it is the acting upon the potentiality, it is the taking of the advice lovingly given by Beings of Light that begins the process of actualizing these impulses, these potentialities and this advice. And so I must convey to you the reader the importance of actually conducting the experiments and absorbing the material, working it into your lives on a daily basis.

The magical perspective is simply a special way of looking at your world. This perspective empowers you the reader with the forces of manifestation that you have denied for so many generations on your world. Now there were ages in what you would call your "past" that the magical perspective was appreciated by the majority of the people. Your "myths" - though I do not like the word myths, for it denotes that these events did not transpire, for indeed they DID transpire for the most part - depict those eras in human evolution when humankind took the responsibility of personal manifestation quite seriously. Currently, in what you term "the aboriginal systems," the magical perspective is appreciated and practiced. However, it is usually only utilized by a select caste of revered leaders who are endowed by the members of the collective with the magical powers.

Dialogue - The Magician of Old
4/22/04 4:18 pm

Seth - Now Mark, the Scientist of Consciousness IS the magician of old. They are one and the same. You may use this or not, but we are essentially teaching the reader, by way of the Scientist of Consciousness model, to use "natural" forces to create desired realities. This is magic my friend. I think that if we keep this as more of a subtext than overt, we can intrigue the reader into coming with us on this journey. This is, I must add, "divine magic" we are describing: Reality Creation in collaboration with All That Is, the energy source for ALL creation. Ideas of mistrust of spirituality, as if it were not powerful or not legitimate, fall away when the ultimate power of All That Is is felt in your experiments as a Scientist of Consciousness. Try it Mark.

First Scientists
The Scientist of Consciousness is the magician of old. The magician, the shaman, the witch: these forbearers of

96

humanity's spiritual traditions were your world's <u>first</u> scientists. It was only later, when the outer senses replaced the Inner Senses as a means of investigation and exploration - the accumulation of "facts" for their own sake, the acquiring of knowledge without meaning - that the scientist's role became de-spiritualized, secularized and developed into what it is today.

The work at hand is to spiritualize and make sacred the experiences of humans on Earth at this time, through collaborations with Beings of Light. Now I do not mean to offend when I exclude organized religions from this discussion. If you are getting what you need from your religion, by all means continue. That is my advice to you. However, if you feel that your evolution as a Soul is stagnant and you are not getting what you need from your religion to see you through the coming transformation, then I would advise you to try the methods in this book. Keep your religious affiliation and use these ideas as an adjunct to your practice.

There is much good in the mainstream religions and there are opportunities in all of them to achieve the enlightened state necessary to make the transition into the Fourth Dimension. Unfortunately, these opportunities are often hidden under the great weight of dogma and misconception that clouds meaning and disempowers the individual. This is why I counsel you the reader, to accept nothing into your heart that goes against your very nature as a child born in love out of the creative power of All That Is. Make up your own mind. Think for your own self. Accept no ideas, including the ideas in this book, if your intuitive voice tells you they are not right for You-the-Soul.

Magician Shaman Witch

Astral Travel, time travel, projections of consciousness - these are various terms describing essentially a single activity: the use of human consciousness in a focused way. If you look at the various descriptions of the activities of let us say, a magician, a shaman or a witch, you would find distinctions made between the various activities. Yet if you were to compare these activities across the board, you would see that all three are attempting to accomplish similar goals, for similar reasons, in similar ways. Ultimately, all are making use of the human consciousness to create changes - changes in personal and shared Reality Fields.

Dear Reader, when you conduct your experiments, you will find you have the most control in your own Personal Reality Field. You will be investigating within your radius of manifestation. Yet over time, as you become proficient in the use of intention in the creation of Reality Constructs, it becomes easy to expand your potential field of manifestation to include related or contiguous fields. Now, because all is one and everything is related, you can have effects on anything in your consensus reality. All you need is the focus and power in the moment. This is the vehicle for healing others at a distance, for example. It takes some time and experience to get acquainted with these networks of creation, or "gridworks" as I have described them in earlier manuscripts. However, any one of you can master the workings of these fields and grids. Turn to the experiments at the end of this chapter for more information.

Dialogue - Karma
3/24/04 12:30 pm

Mark - *Relating to your model of humans as co-creators of our realities with All That Is, where does Karma come in, if at all?*

Seth - *Mark, as you may remember, I do not like the word karma. It is a facet of the dogma of an Eastern religion. The truth about the human Soul is that there is no karma, there are only experiences. One experiences one's lessons in materialized form that one comes to Earth to experience. These experiences run the gamut of what you could consider as "positive" or "negative" and you keep returning to these experiences in human form until you have mastered your lessons. Karma entails, in the general Western, popular definition, some sort of "dues paying" left over from supposed "past lives" that one endures in the current life. But since all lives are simultaneous, these sorts of definitions lose meaning. If you attribute a brick falling on your foot in this life to your karma from a past life, you are greatly oversimplifying an essentially sacred, or should I say soulful or spiritual experience. The Eastern religions are closer to the truth of the evolution of the Soul than the Christian religions. However, no religion has yet explained it in terms useful enough for humans to comprehend it in its totality, and by so doing receive the divine information that would unlock the heart. No, you have been blocked in your spiritual evolution by your egos. It is now time to relax your egos and let your Souls shine through.*

Natural Magic

In my book with my First Subject, *The Magical Approach*, we covered the broad concept of man and woman as magician. The magical way is simply an appreciation for conscious manifestation in the natural world. You are a part of the natural world. As I have said many times before, you are co-creators with All That Is of all that you observe in your reality. Now, this is a magical process in that you create seemingly something out of nothing. Referring back to my concept of Consciousness Units, you use the "material" of CUs with your free will and intent to create your shared consensus reality. Telepathy is operative on all levels and so you have a cohesive illusion; a manifestation of your world and your Universe that all of you can agree upon. It does look quite real, does it not? Yet if you believe what I have been telling you over these many years, this "enduring" physical reality of yours is really just "a bunch of hot air." It falls apart under the kind of scrutiny I am asking you to muster as a Scientist of Consciousness.

Dialogue - Conscious Co-Creation with CUs
3/23/04 8:30 am

Mark - Seth, I could use some advice on the conscious use of Consciousness Units to co-create the life I want, particularly with regards to my house and land.

Seth - Mark, the key word here is <u>conscious</u>. You are correct. You and your fellow humans co-create your lives "unconsciously" for the most part. This is the result of the amnesia I spoke of earlier, so that you forget the love and are more inclined to learn your lessons. Now the amnesia is being lifted, and you are becoming aware of the true nature of your reality. So it is a matter of habit. Make your use of CUs <u>conscious</u> on a moment-to-moment point basis. This is easily done, is it not? Whenever you find yourself varying from your thought-path, nudge yourself back. You have done this a few times this morning already. Negativity will try to draw you toward its own path. That is what it does in your reality. Your task at hand is to redirect negativity's energy into creating love and confidence in the moment. The CUs that comprise Mark and his environment are fluid in the moment. They can go either way, positive or negative, depending on your subconscious or conscious intent. So Mark, keep the scales on the positive side consciously and watch your positive manifestations of house and land - prosperity - be created in these moments.

Healthy Wealthy Wise

My Third Subject has adopted a saying from one of your Earth's cultural traditions. It is a blessing one wishes for one's self and others: healthy, wealthy, wise. These three elements of life are the focus of many in your world. Perhaps we can use this blessing as an example of how you can, with consistent intention and application, co-create with All That Is, your greatest potential for health, prosperity, and wisdom. Now, you are all individual humans on your great Earth, each with your separate, idiosyncratic propensities for growth - evolution - on all levels of manifestation in the physical and other dimensional realms. Therefore, it should seem obvious that one human's health, wealth and wisdom might certainly not be another's. Having said that, let us examine the powerful, evocative ideas and beliefs suggested in the three words.

Health is a topic we could easily spend an entire book on discussing and indeed I have done just that with my First Subject. *(The Way Toward Health. mf)* Those of you who know the circumstances of that writing, know that my collaboration with her ended with that book. She made The Transition into her Home Dimension. Now some may say that it is odd to write a book about health with suggestions for creating health in the physical body, and the author does not survive the writing of the book. Let us simply say that my First Subject had her reasons for her behaviors, as do you all. There is physical health, there is mental health and there is spiritual health. There are lessons to be learned in all three realms for all of you as you make your journeys into physical reality. What might appear confusing to your eyes as you judge another, may be simply the other's decision to learn their lessons in their unique fashion. I should note that I am still in communication with my First Subject and that she finds this topic of her death a source of great amusement. This Entity felt as though she was leaving physical life with a sense of great irony, focused as she was on the production of a book on health. She was demonstrating for all her readers, the truth regarding The Transition from the physical into the etheric. Now she trusts that the readers of that book may understand the irony and the pathos inherent in that death.

Creating Health

Creating health ... I will be extremely brief, though some may doubt that I can BE brief (humorously). Your health is the most evident aspect of your Personal Reality creation, for you create your physical body and its "conditions" just as surely as you create the rest of what we have been referring to as your Personal Reality Field. Now you ARE experiencing your physical body created through the template you chose before your birth. This template provided you with a body that holds "built in" lessons for you to experience. The lessons of the physical body are myriad and continue until your physical death. Yet on a basic level, relative to all other humans, if you are experiencing a happy, healthy mental environment, you may be in all probability co-creating with All That Is, a happy, healthy body. If you are entertaining negative thoughts of disease and low self-worth, you may be in all likelihood creating a body that will experience that level of dis-ease. This happens unconsciously for the most part, this creation of healthy or non-healthy bodily conditions. Sometimes though you can catch yourself responding to your own or another human's "offer" to create a disease state in your own apparatus. For example: if you respond to a statement such as, " I'm catching a cold," by saying to this person, "Yes, I'm catching a cold too," you are creating the bodily conditions to receive the cold. This is material we have covered elsewhere and so I shall not digress.

Now there are those of you who are experiencing your current lives with challenges, such as a lack of arms, legs, various organs and so on. There are also some physical diseases that may seem to be "beyond healing." Within your Third-Dimensional world, it is indeed thought to be impossible to grow a new limb or new organ, or to recover from a "terminal" illness. However, you are headed for a realization that ALL of the maladies and illnesses of humankind may be corrected through proper use of the imagination and the sacred powers of manifestation with All That Is. In the Fourth Dimension your thoughts will be instantly manifested into Reality Constructs without the lag-time in between that you currently experience in Third-Dimensional reality. Should you have self-created "incurable" illnesses and physical challenges, you may learn your lessons through resolving these Soul issues with your powerful thoughts of healing. These are simply some of the more profound experiences that await you in the post-transition Fourth-Dimensional reality.

Natural Healing

To continue on this line of thought - that of exploring the possibility of healing all wounds, physical, spiritual and mental - let me elaborate on a concept we may refer to as Natural Healing. By this type of healing, I mean allowing the body to heal itself with the aid of "soft" technologies. These soft technologies do not include surgery or drugs but do include some age-old therapies and some natural products of the Earth: hypnosis or "healing talk," and the application of various plants, minerals, waters, oils etc. This system I am describing to you is of ancient origins. It is the basis of ALL of your modern medicine. The simplest way to describe this is to say that the human body is a natural organism - it is a creation from the natural elements of your Earth by your divinely-inspired consciousness. And from the beginning of your time on Earth, healing talk has been used by your healers to effect healing changes within human beings. So does it not make sense that you may repair or renew the organism in a natural way, with natural methods and products?

But where to begin? Do you have to seek out systems of correspondence, looking for the leaf or oil that will bring relief of a corresponding ailment? Not necessarily. When we approach this activity from a magical perspective, <u>any</u> natural remedy will do. You may make your own associations between the remedy and the condition, in effect personalizing this divine activity. You do it with your thoughts, again, and you imbue the activity of healing with emotion - strong emotion - which is the electromagnetic healing force in this endeavor. Now this naturally requires a profound trust in your own abilities to choose and to empower the remedy with curative powers. But this is entirely within the potential of all human beings to accomplish. It may be conceived of as a form of self-hypnosis while perhaps reminding yourself that you are a Soul with a Body rather than a Body with a Soul. Within the etheric domain of the Soul, all is possible, including the healing of all ailments.

Dialogue - DREAM - Havingness
5/17/04 6:26 am

Mark - I just had a strange dream. Could you help me interpret it?
Seth - If you wish. Now, I am aware of the dream and it is good that you wrote down what you remember of it. You are quite correct in your feelings that the overall dream concerns your beliefs about "having." In other words, it was a symbolized drama presenting you with your lesson for this current life on prosperity, abundance, havingness. You are also correct in your interpretation that you have some problems with the prospect of wealth, that is, having

your OWN nice home. You feel in the dream as if you were transported into the home unwillingly and now you have to explain yourself. In other words you are saying, "What is a poor person like me doing in such a nice house?" This is the element in your personality that you must overcome before you can ACCEPT the new wealth and prosperity that you are asking for. This is a repeating dream, because you have been having this conversation with yourself over-and-over, over many years. "Do I deserve to have a nice house? Why must I always be a resident in other people's homes as a renter?" In your dream world you are working out these issues. Currently it seems you are coming into a realization that you may be able to have your dream house. The couple in your dream may literally represent the wealthy couple that you will meet shortly and take into the business as benefactors, without a desire for personal monetary reward. They do not need the money Mark. They are demonstrating for you the attitude of wealth, without arrogance, without disdain for those less fortunate, with extreme confidence and love. Mark, your mission (humorously) seems to be, at this time in your development, to adopt this strategy of embodying love and confidence in all that you do, but particularly with the publishing and distribution of our books and with your beginning lectures and demonstrations on this channeling phenomenon we are creating together, you and I. That is all for now.

(As Seth described, I found myself within my dream environment, unwillingly projected into a luxury home. The occupants were a couple - a man and woman - that I recognized from earlier dream experiences. I was ashamed of my involuntary trespassing in their home. Seth is right that the dream revealed my feelings about prosperity and shame and a host of other issues. Look to the Q&A section for more of Seth's comments on my "prosperity sequence." mf)

Creating Prosperity

Now we shall turn to matters of prosperity. Let us proceed from the beginning. The first step is an assessment, a self-assessment if you will. You first must assess what level of abundance you wish to achieve. You then assess the current level of havingness and examine the difference between the two. This difference between what you have and what you wish to have, can serve as the emotional impetus or motivation to create or manifest the desired result. There is no manifestation without emotional content. The greater the emotional intensity or desire, the more quickly and surely the manifestation occurs.

You create your reality. You are magicians in this respect and it would be good to be more intentional in this magical view of things: creating consciously, with a positive perspective for the good of not only yourself, but for all others, all of humankind. This deference to the sum of all humanity holds the key to effective conscious manifestation for you, Dear Reader. In effect, you are demonstrating your commitment to the good of all with these intentions. The Divine Logos that is All That Is holds you to this commitment to all, as a condition of progressing on your developmental path, your path of Soul Evolution. Now if this indeed sounds fantastic and perhaps unworthy of consideration, let that egoic response serve as the measure of your distance from Soul. Now you know how far you have to go in this enterprise.

Your personal manifestation of your current level of prosperity or abundance is an important indicator of what your beliefs are with regards to havingness. This is the feedback I have been describing to you in this book: the reflection of your mental environment that IS your Personal Reality Field. Often you may notice that there is a direct relationship between giving and prosperity; for in the natural perspective - the magical view of things - there IS a give-and-take at the foundation of your manifestation activities. You can see this in the breath of life or in the "pulse" of your natural reality. Just as the breath is cyclical, with the inhalation and then the exhalation followed by a pause, the pulse of life or manifestation is cyclical with a pre-manifestation period followed by a pause and the manifestation. The completion of one cycle may take much less than a microsecond in your perceived time. This is still long enough to give the "appearance" of physicality or "bedrock reality," as some call it.

As you begin to get a feel for this pulsation of ideas into constructs, powered by the Consciousness Units with electromagnetic properties, you will also begin to gain conscious control of your creativity in the moment. This manifestation cycle is the framework upon which your camouflage reality is built. This pulse can be experienced under specific circumstances. You may, as I describe in an experiment at this end of this chapter, using your inherent powers of creativity, slow down the progression of time within your Personal Reality Field. You do this with your intention, using your Inner Senses. Time is felt as elastic with the use of these Inner Senses, and slowing time down to the microsecond level may reveal this breath of life we have been discussing. You may also observe how your thoughts create and support the various aspects of your Personal Reality Field.

Now to simplify for the reader, let us discuss a distillation of some of the natural elements of manifestation related to goodness and giving. There is much good to be had in the giving of money, personal items, your time, etc. Holding-on to your "things" or being miserly with your time or money creates a state of consciousness that is not conducive to prosperity. This may already be quite apparent. You may be miserly and have the "appearance" of prosperity, yet you may not enjoy it for you have not shared it with others. And by creating your "mental estate" on a foundation of stinginess and greed, are you really expecting to create lasting abundance? Better to create a foundation of sharing and love for yourself and others, intentionally. The positive creates upon the positive for the good of all here. The Reality Constructs take hold and are tempered in a telepathic mental environment of trust and love. Others with similar loving strategies of manifestation will be drawn to you in support of this beneficial world-view. This is the beginning of the loving, self-sustaining communities that will reshape your world.

Lessons and Wisdom

Now wisdom comes from lessons learned in all of the domains of human interaction. I have mentioned the physical, the mental and the spiritual domains, to establish lines of discussion for us as we attempt to make ourselves understood. Naturally, these realms of understanding must surely overlap in some instances in the lives of individuals. You will likely discover where these domains merge as you conduct your experiments in the field.

To be healthy, in terms of these domains of learning, would imply that certain standards of creative manifestation would be consistently met within the overall context of the particular body you are using in the current incarnation. The powers of creative thought with which you create the body and the world around the body have great leeway in creating health and disease according to lessons to be learned. For example: you may be currently incarnated in a body that has defects from birth. Still, you may enjoy a high degree of physical health, relative to others who have no defects. Here we enter into the area of Value Fulfillment that I have described in previous manuscripts. It is not easy to assess any particular individual's incarnational learning experiences using flimsy surface indicators. For example: a human with a major facial or other disfigurement might elicit a responding emotion of pity from another. Yet the Soul Self of this human may wear the disfigurement as "a badge of honor." For Souls may CHOOSE these types of lives to learn their lessons quickly, due to the high-emotionality involved in living a life with a severe disfigurement. Here, the value of living with honor and acceptance within a disabled physical form is explored in earnest. Soul Wisdom is earned through such a life lived.

Now the opposite, of course, is also true. Lessons regarding living a "charmed life" are in store for all who inhabit the Third-Dimension. All That Is seeks to know through the experience of Souls, both the exalted and the mundane. No experience is better or worse than another. Again I refer you to discussions of Value Fulfillment in my older books for more light on this matter. The following experiments may help you more fully comprehend these important concepts.

Experiment - Slowing Down Time
Hypothesis: you may effectively slow down time for study or for other practical purposes

Using your Inner Senses as exploratory tools, you may conduct your experiments free from what you might refer to as "the constraints of time." You know that the past and future are created now, in this Moment Point. You may use your conscious intent to imbue your Moment Points with an "elasticity" that can afford you greater leeway in your studies. For example: you may through your intention create a "slowing down" of time within your Personal Reality Field. Now you have undoubtedly already experienced this slowing down of time while engaged in an activity that you know well, an activity in which you are completely absorbed. Time slows down in such circumstances. So let us suppose you wished to cover a broad range of activities in a meditation session, for example, and you have only a few minutes to do so. Before your meditation, simply give your Energy Personality your intention to expand time for the moment, or slow it down, to enable you to complete your activities. This is especially effective for those who are on self-healing regimens. You can intend to deliver several hours of self-healing suggestions to yourself in the space of just a few minutes. Your Higher Self or Energy Personality will then carry it out. You have used your free will to choose this activity.

Conduct Your Ritual of Sanctuary

Induce a relaxed state in your physical body by whatever means suits you. When you are relaxed, consider the Inner Senses counterparts to your physical senses of sight, touch, smell, hearing and taste. As you do, you may notice that these Inner Senses make themselves known to you in a somewhat "dreamy" fashion. What I am saying is that these senses have a quality of duration and intensity unlike the physical

senses of the outer world. Your perception of Inner Hearing, for example, may be perceived as though each sound resonated within your consciousness. This might be somewhat similar to the sounds you hear as you are falling asleep. The sounds seem to be extended, as though time were slowing down. For purposes of this experiment, this is exactly the perceptive state I am asking you to create. Simply utilize your imagination to "turn on" the Inner Senses with an eye towards the slowing down of time within and without. The seeing on the inward eye is slowing down. The sounds are slowing down. Perhaps even your sense of how your skin feels in contact with the air around you and the surface of your chair or pillow begins to deepen and lengthen. Now when you have slowed down time within your Personal Reality Field in this fashion, present to your awareness your healing suggestions, your questions or what have you, with the intention that resolution will be found, thanks to the slowing down of time you have created. This alteration of your perceptive field may also give you insights into the uses and powers of your Inner Senses.
Findings - Document your findings after each experiment.

Experiment - Dream Interpretation
Hypothesis: the energy personality can read and interpret your dream symbols

As in the previous Dialogue, write down what you remember of a dream upon awakening from sleep.

Conduct Your Ritual of Sanctuary

When you are next in contact with your Energy Personality through meditation or other rituals of contact, ask for an interpretation of the dream with regards to your particular symbols. Within a context of learning your lessons and understanding your own dreams, your Energy Personality can help with interpretation. Typically, your Energy Personality will not resort to revelations that may interfere with the learning of lessons.

Findings - Document your findings in whatever form you find best-suited to this endeavor.

Experiment - Healthy Wealthy Wise

Hypothesis: through intention improvements can be made in your health, havingness and learning

We have covered the means to these improvements in this previous chapter. Generally, it is a good idea to have a richly visualized image of what you would like to create with regards to health, wealth and wisdom. As in the previous suggestions in these matters, the image should virtually resonate with the desired thoughts and emotions that you would experience on having created and perceived the manifested Reality Constructs. It may help to create a piece of art that helps to focus the creative energies.

Conduct Your Ritual of Sanctuary

With your art piece or your written manifesto or other focusing objects at hand, enter into a relaxed state of consciousness. Here you are asking for the natural energies of the world to assist you in creating your improvements. In a sense, you are using these energies of transformation to imbue the focusing objects with generative power on the small level to create the desired outcomes on the larger level. You are providing the emotional charge through your visualization to drive into creation the Reality Constructs you have in mind. You will know when the changes have been made, as you may feel an Inner Sense awareness that you have succeeded.

Findings - Document your findings.

Experiment - Natural Healing

Hypothesis: you can heal yourself and others via the etheric gridworks

Since **Seth Speaks** I have spoken of the etheric gridworks that sustain the realities of your Universe. These energetic lattice-works of creation and support are currently unknown to the majority of humans on Earth. Yet again, the natives or aboriginals have used these networks since the beginning of your time to interplay with the natural world around them. So certainly this experiment is simply a means to reintroduce you to a practice that you may have engaged in countless times, in other eras, in other bodies.

Conduct Your Ritual of Sanctuary

Utilize your calming practices to access a deep state of relaxation. With your Energy Personality as your guide, ask for guidance as to causes and solutions in these matters of personal health and the health of others. Suggestions may come to you as images, sounds or other sensations. Keeping with the metaphor of a gridwork, you might receive an image of a lattice superimposed over your own body or the body of the subject you are assisting. The area of interest may glow or otherwise make itself known to you. Using whatever means that comes naturally to you, facilitate the transformation of the area of interest into one of integration and support with the rest of the body. This is a personal choice of methods and means that may come into your awareness through your Inner Senses

Later in this series I will speak of the possibility of the reader increasing their vibrational rate and so intentionally moving themselves out of a "disease" state and into a state of health. This is done in collaboration with your Energy Personality. You may experience your current state of illness within the dream reality and so learn your lesson there instead of in Third-Dimensional reality within your current timeframe. Our third book in this series will have more on this subject. If you are currently at a stage of Soul Evolution that would enable you to experiment with these probabilities, please do so in a systematic way, with guidance from your Energy Personality and with attention to the requirements of experimentation as a Scientist of Consciousness.

Findings - Document your findings, perhaps with drawings and ideas for future experiments.

CHAPTER SIX

Cultivating the Human Virtues

Dialogue - CPA & Depression
4/22/04 3:25 pm

Mark - Consecutive Positive Assessments, momen-to-moment: this was your remedy for negative thoughts and realities that you described in a personal session. How do you begin this program of positive assessment, if let's say, you're depressed?

Seth - An excellent question Mark. The answer is related to the one I gave you concerning your house and land. It is a matter of the power differential with respect to your relationship with your world. Depression is largely a matter of powerlessness accepted as a reality - a field of reality - by the individual. As a field, it colors the entire existence and all DOES INDEED <u>seem</u> hopeless. Now, just as I advised you Mark, to unlock your conditioning and take back your power from people and institutions, so too do I advise the so-called "depressed" person to rise up and make the ges-

ture of transcendence into the Realm of Power. All it takes is one charged Moment Point of personal responsibility for your evolution, to push the balance out of stasis into change: positive change for the individual. Then you simply place further Moment Points of personal responsibility for your growth and positive assessments and behaviors, "one in front of the other," to create the positive future. Now, should the negative energies make a comeback, it does require the individual to reaffirm a commitment to a positive future, <u>in that moment</u>, and once again push the manifestation chain of creative moments out of stasis and into the positive. The Negative Reality is rejected and the Positive Field of Reality is accepted once again. Do I make myself clear?

Mark - *It's getting clearer and clearer. Thanks Seth.*

Seth - *As an addendum, Mark. Remember too, that in these moments you are affecting all of your Simultaneous Lives. So certainly you are doing your <u>selves</u> much good via these positive assessments. And perhaps I should mention the obvious - that just as the Accepted Negative Field of Reality experienced by the "depressed" person has momentum and continuity in a morbid, yet familiar sense, so too does the Accepted Field of Positive Emotions and Behaviors hold its own momentum, continuity, and familiarity in a positive, even joyful sense. Do you understand?*

Mark - *Yes Seth. That last point carries a lot of hope I think.*

Spontaneity

The concept of spontaneity can further our discussion of creating the Personal Reality Field. To be spontaneous, according to one of your Earthly definitions, is to act without forethought, willy-nilly, according to the present moment's frivolous inclinations. Now I may be casting this term in a negative light somewhat, yet is it not true that spontaneity has a "bad reputation" in your culture. To be spontaneous is thought to be somewhat reckless and unthinking, is it not? The spontaneous are thought to be irresponsible, in many ways, and lacking in maturity and good judgment.

If you have been following this discussion in my new books, you may have noticed that I am a big fan of spontaneity, and the accompanying practice of recognizing and "following" life-affirming impulses. But for now, let us investigate how the practice of spontaneity may have earned such a bad reputation in your culture. To begin, the founders of your American nation were of a strong puritanical bent. They were hard-working, intensely religious humans, who were taught that "idle hands are the devil's playground." So the natural spontaneous behavior of humans enjoying the moment, even of children in many cases, during those seminal years of occupation in your country, was discouraged.

Now this is speaking of the U.S. only here. Other nations had obviously different beginnings, yet some <u>were</u> similar. So you, as a people, were not generated from hedonistic loins, in other words. Your culture has proceeded from day one until the present on a decidedly anti-pleasure trajectory, admittedly with a few pleasure-seeking counter-culture movements in between. So given this history it is no surprise that, for the most part, Americans are not a spontaneous lot. This type of behavior is not rewarded in a society that values business interests and profit-taking over positive human development. Currently, as a culture, the U.S .has entered an era of warlike anti-pleasure such as your modern Earth has never seen. Surprisingly, many of your citizens appear to accept this state of belligerence and negativity, if one is to believe the many polls that are taken and the results proclaimed to the world.

For now, let me simply suggest an alternative to the anti-pleasure movement in your country. This would be the search for pleasure within your Personal Reality and the creation of pleasure through the acknowledgment of and acting on pleasurable, life-affirming impulses. These are behaviors that may lead you to experience the feeling of being supported like a beloved child on a wave of ecstasy that is indeed the embodiment of All That Is.

Now let us clear up some of the misconceptions some may have of spontaneity with a description of "true spontaneity." We need look no further for a graphic example of true spontaneity than the experience of accessing one's Inner Senses and learning one's lessons. The first requirement for this communication is a lowering of the ego defenses: that quality of mind that protects and defends one's beliefs and one's world view against "attack" from differing beliefs and differing world views. The ego must release its strangle hold on the physical perceptions before divine information - spontaneous impulses - can be adequately perceived with the Inner Senses, and then acted upon if appropriate. So true spontaneity is ultimately profoundly responsible and ethical at its base. True spontaneity is not necessarily the actions of the "free spirit," however, in your terms. This aspect relates to the terms "Young Soul" and "Old Soul" that we discussed in Volume One. Let us go further here. The idea of a free spirit, in your culture and other of the world's cultures, who acts on every whim that comes to mind, is not the spontaneous spirit I am describing. True spontaneity requires discernment as to which impulses within consciousness to act on to further the learning of lessons for oneself and for the higher good of everyone else. This is critical. The awakening human learns their lessons consciously and with courage, relishing the life experience whatever the "conditions," positive, negative or in between, in your terms. Then, as I said, contributing to the consensus manifestation in positive, life-affirming ways, always.

Now further... you are awakening, some of you, within lives that some would call "miserable." Some of you will use your formidable powers in collaboration with All That Is to heighten your vibrational rate in this lifetime and bring an end to your miseries. Yet some of you will live out your lives in these subjectively named "miserable conditions," knowing that you are fulfilling your contract with yourself, and learning your lessons for your Soul Self and for All That Is. Both of the examples I have just described are becoming fully awakened and finding pleasure there, yet only they know this on a Soul level. Again, to outside observers it would appear that some are trapped in their misery. If one were to look closer though, perhaps one would see the spark of Soul wisdom in the eyes of those I am speaking about. You are all involved in a complex dramatic presentation for the benefit of yourselves and All That Is.

Negative Thinking

An excellent question in these matters might be, "If negative thoughts and images lead to the creation of negative events, and these events are painful, why do people continue in the creation of negative thoughts?" I have covered this before and I now will elaborate on this paradox. Why would a human continue to think and imagine the negative and create negative Reality Constructs and thus feel the negative emotions that come with the negative manifestation? In a way, the reason for this unusual behavior is that many of the negative reality creators are so accustomed to creating from their negative, repetitive thoughts and beliefs that they essentially know of no other ways to think and feel. The creation of their negative personal realities has become "a force of nature," to coin one of your phrases. The force is quite powerful and has become personalized over time so that the human is entranced with these thoughts and behaviors, thinking there is absolutely no other possible way to think and behave.

Sometimes under these circumstances of entranced negativity, the only way out is through a reincarnational drama or lesson. The Higher Self of the individual creates a life-or-death struggle to divert the attention away from the increasingly negative and self-defeating manifestations. The human, then, is often quite relieved to enter into a different creative opportunity, even though it might entail a serious illness, accident, mental crisis and so on. The diversion has the effect of waking up the individual from the trance of negativity. They then see the world with a new-found clarity. They have a sudden appreciation and sense of gratitude for life where before they were living a robotic existence. These creative opportunities may result in the death of the physical form. Still, the Soul experiences that result as a success, for the human has encountered and met the challenge in their own way. This is the lesson they were to learn, and whatever was learned is now part of the knowledge of the individual Soul, the Entity and All That Is. Of course, there is the probability you may avoid the life-or-death drama by approaching your lessons "head on," and not avoiding them - learning what you have come to Earth to learn. The free will choice is always yours.

Loving Understanding

Let us now discuss loving understanding, one of the great virtues of humankind. Now there is love and there is love. It would seem that each of you might have your own definition for what love means. Let me tell you my definition:

"love of another is acceptance of another regardless of how the other appears, speaks or behaves." This aspect of love comes from understanding what the human purpose is on your great Earth. Generally, the purpose is to co-create with All That Is a life of learning. You are on the planet to learn from your experiences in your particular niche in your personal environment. When you can appreciate this overriding fact of life, you can come to a loving understanding of ANYONE you meet upon your Earth. You are ALL on the same voyage: that of the path to Soul Realization. Each person you meet in your experiences is a teacher for you, therefore, and from these interactions you learn your lessons and your knowledge grows. Now, All That Is also grows in knowledge and experience with you, as you co-create and then experience your lessons. All That Is is the energy source for all of creation. Indeed, you are on your Earth to experience for All That Is, your life lessons that include EVERY MOMENT in your existence. Each second of your waking and dreaming hours provides learning opportunities for You-the-Soul. This is true for not only your current life in this timeframe, but for all your many lives in this and other timeframes past, present and future. This is not to minimize the importance of any given life. It is simply a fact of life, Dear Reader. And when you understand this in its most profound sense, you can begin to have this sense of loving understanding I am describing, for yourself as well as for others.

Collective Manifestation

So in a word, love is the answer. If you were to live your life as a poet, a romantic poet let us say, one that was immersed in love, and indeed unable to sense or formulate a single thought that was not love, imagine how LOVING your existence would be. But instead many of you focus on murders, such as you have in your negative media; personal vendettas, such as you are engaged-in at the workplace; and general cynical gossiping, such as makes up the Moment-to-Moment Points of your ongoing lives. This is not to paint all of you with the same brush, but you must take responsibility for whatever part you play in the creation of negative Reality Constructs in your world. If you contribute a negative thought, you are partly responsible for the collective negative manifestation. If you contribute a negative gesture, you are partly responsible for the collective negative manifestation. It makes sense, does it not, given what I have described to you about the nature of your reality? If you become angry at a person of a different color while driving your automobile and shout at them and gesture at them in an obscene way, you are responsible for your part in the collective negative manifestation of racial prejudice in your current timeframe. Does this not make sense to you? If you scream in anger at your child, you are responsible for the collective manifestation of child abuse in your timeframe. It is quite logical in its consistency. You may believe that if you commit these violations in private, that they do not count, because no one is observing your behavior. But telepathy, as I said before, is operative at all levels. You ALL know what is "on your minds." You feel that you have to pretend that you DON'T know, however, to maintain your private lives. Yet all of this will be out in the open soon, and I would urge you to clean up your thoughts and behaviors so that you will not be caught in the habitual negative thinking and behaviors that currently hold you back.

Belief Change

And when you look at your Personal Reality and see a change, one that reflects a change in your beliefs, and perhaps it feels uncomfortable to acknowledge it because it feels so foreign to you, let that serve as validation that you are on the right path. For example: where once there was fear of a particular group or race and there is now acceptance and growing affection, let that serve as validation that your Soul is evolving in beneficial ways.

No, you cannot err on the side of too much love. You cannot have too much affection for your fellow humans. My advice to you is to practice loving one another WITH ALL OF YOUR MIGHT. The emotional content, highly-charged, is what helps the new reality break through the old, and establish itself as the new manifestation, "the New World." I continually encourage Mark to be ruthlessly loving and confident, and I suggest that also to the reader of these words. Continually, moment-to-moment, create your world through a perception of love and confidence. You can be a model for those who need this guidance, in how to think, feel and act.

For those of you who can accept such responsibilities, your growing skills with the use of the Non-Physical Senses and your growing knowledge of how to use the powers of love and confidence, can thrust you to the fore-front of the movement of human beings who are seeking their own enlightenment and the Soul progression also of the species.

If You Want Peace

With an appreciation for loving understanding and the power of this state of consciousness to transform fear and anger, comes the possibility for peace. Dear Reader, if you want peace, you can have peace. Make it with your thoughts. If you want the wars to cease, you can create that with your thoughts. It all begins with your loving intention in the moment. Your thoughts of peace and loving understanding coalesce on the subtle levels, to create their counterparts in physical reality. What is the counterpart to peace, love and understanding? A physical world where WAR IS NOT TOLERATED BY THE PEOPLE. War cannot be sustained on a diet of peace and loving understanding. War perishes in such circumstances. And as war and violence fade into memory, new, positive life-affirming Reality Constructs are thrust into your world with the energy of the loving thoughts, the peaceful thoughts, the thoughts of understanding and acceptance for your fellow human beings.

Your Reality is Feedback

You see, your Personal Reality Field is literally feedback of your ongoing mental activities. You can always look at your created reality to see how you are doing. This of course assumes that you are aware of your lessons and are not denying the spiritual, or need I say, "metaphysical" underpinnings of your so-called "physical" life. If you feel you haven't enough information as to what your lessons are, the next time you are in communication with your Energy Personality, simply ask for guidance as to what your lessons might be in this incarnation and wait for the reply. You will get a direct reply telepathically if it is appropriate information for you to have at the time, or you may be presented with a "graphic example" by way of a reincarnational drama or comedy in your physical world. These events present your lessons in stark relief against the background of your mundane, robotic existence. You will recognize these as "teaching moments" or "moments of awakening" by their surprising appropriateness and synchronous attributes. Again, as I have stated previously, you will know it when you see it for YOU HAVE CREATED IT, for purposes of your own learning and Soul Evolution.

For example: you may have noticed a teaching moment in your own life that was not tragic in the least but amusing and profound. Perhaps you have had the experience of being the center of the cosmic joke, when everything around you was turned against you in humorous and symbolic ways. Certainly all of you have had these experiences, yet they are too easy to dismiss as coincidence. These are your reincarnational comedies - teaching moments of the absurd and ironic. Now within these teaching moments, you also have the opportunity for creating loving understanding out of negative emotions - embarrassment and shame, anger and fear - just as you have the opportunity for transformation within the reincarnational <u>dramas</u> of your life. Simply note that these episodes of dramatic and comedic teaching moments represent opportunities for IMMEDIATE TRANSFORMATION, IMMEDIATE SOUL GROWTH. I advise you the reader of this book to take advantage of these experiences, therefore, when they arise.

Dialogue - Converting Negative Thoughts
4/9/04 4:50 pm

Mark - Any comments on the current negative state of reality in this timeframe?

Seth - Some comments... by expressing negative thoughts about the war or anything, you are colluding with the Negative Forces. Make the effort to deal with these issues in love. Love is the strongest of all energies in the Universe. Focus on the love that you can feel for everyone, including the "war people." The only way to convince the haters is to model unconditional love in all your actions. Mark, be a peacemaker by converting your negativity into love and by turning hatred into its opposite. This skill is what will convert people to the peace-

ful side, and this skill is what will allow you to stay in the
Fourth Dimension. So practice, practice, practice.

Consecutive Positive Assessments

In your world currently, you as a race are experiencing the disintegration of the fundamental structures that hold your societies together. It is easy for you to see this phenomenon in your Western world, for your media proclaim the disasters and upheavals within your institutions on a daily basis. I refer to these media as the "negative media," for obvious reasons. In a very real sense, your media shape and negatively spin the events of your world to depict the basest interpretations, appealing to the lowest aspects of humankind. Because there are very few alternative voices in your media network, the media as a whole tend to reinforce and perpetuate negative experiences in the minds of humanity.

Those of you who wish to go into the Unity of Consciousness Dimension "with your eyes wide open," would do well to divorce yourselves from all forms of negative media. I have explained in Volume One how the violent images and stories serve to trigger biochemical responses in your bodies, so that you are conditioned to continue watching, reading or listening. It becomes an addiction in time, so that you become "hooked" on negativity. You become hooked on the adrenaline that is released within your bodies.

Remembering what I have described to you concerning the activities of the Negative Entities as they seek out fear and anxiety, perhaps the reader can see how a daily diet of this - such as violent movies, newscasts and the like - could increasingly attract the Negative Forces, until there is not room within your mental environment for love, compassion or the other human virtues.

"But how Seth," you might ask, "can I protect myself from these media if they surround me in my physical environment? They are everywhere and I must confront them every second of my life just to go out and do my job, go to school, go to church etc. etc. etc." I appreciate your dilemma and I have an answer for you…

Experiment - Consecutive Positive Assessments
Hypothesis: positively assessing all that you experience creates the positive future

In addition to enacting your Ritual of Sanctuary before you go out into your world, I suggest you practice positively assessing everything that comes your way in your existence. Practice until it becomes a matter of fact - a positive habit that you practice ongoing throughout each and every day. Perhaps an experiment is in order here. Again, this builds upon exercises covered in my first book. .

Let us say that you are about to begin your day. You have awakened from sleep, you have opened your eyes and you are perhaps walking to the bathroom.
Perform Your Ritual of Sanctuary
This may be habitual for you now. It should only take a

few seconds to perform your ritual. Then here is where you immediately intervene between the Moment Points of your waking life. In between the moments of remembering and forgetting… you intervene. "It's easy to find the good in each sequential perception." This is your idea for the day. Remembering to conduct your Ritual of Sanctuary; remembering that you create your reality out of your perceived beliefs, ideas and images about your world; remembering to positively assess each sequential perception. Then, do you see how the positive perceptions create the positive future, moment-to-moment? You are rolling out your positive moments before you to create the positive path of your future.

(Thought afterwards - this experiment is especially useful for when you can't avoid the negative media. The reader hopefully will choose not to watch negative TV, violent movies etc. mf)

Findings - Remember to write down your findings from this worthwhile experiment.

Experiment - Transforming Fear and Anger
Hypothesis: you can use your intention to transform fear and anger into courage and loving understanding

Perform your Ritual of Sanctuary.

Think of a fear or anger-creating idea or image that you have been entertaining lately. Surely most of you

134

can come up with an example (humorously). Now that you have it in your mental environment, enliven it with your thoughts and make it seem real. Do this for a few seconds… Now mentally say, "Stop!" and have the intention that you will now turn down the energy on the thought or image, by using your dial or other metaphorical tools, and remind yourself that you are supported on a wave of ecstasy that is indeed your Soul Self. You may consult your Energy Personality or other Guides for help in this matter. When the positive emotions of love and compassion are felt, experience them and relish them for a few seconds. Then end the experiment with your intention to go about your activities, this time experiencing the residual feelings of ecstasy that you will no doubt be enjoying for some time after the experiment.

Findings - Make your notes or remember this use of the Inner Senses for the next potentially fear or anger-producing experience. Document your findings.

CHAPTER SEVEN

The Fourth Dimension and Beyond

Dialogue - Beings of Light
4/13/04 5:00 pm

Mark - When you say that Beings of Light are preparing humanity for these new messages, do you mean that these Spirit Guides are somehow preparing the consciousnesses of their human counterparts?

Seth - Yes Mark, that is what I am suggesting. Humans throughout your world are questioning "on impulse," the fundamental aspects of their realities. Now there will be those who will ask themselves these questions and be astounded to have answers come to them mentally.

Dialogue - Proximity to Seth
4/18/04 8:25 pm

Mark - I sense you wanting to make some comments. Do you?

Seth - Yes Mark... give me a moment. Thank you for creat-

ing an outline into which we can pour our data. The thought you just had that you felt you may have been carried away with creating chapter headings and the like... remember Mark that I am never far from the project. As an inter-dimensional being I can inhabit the space just over your shoulder and watch as you create the material. I am within your consciousness when you let me enter. And so, no not at all. We are collaborating even though you do not feel my presence. When you allow me to accompany you on your outings, by utilizing your free will, you can be sure that I do so...

The Soul Family

You do have many different beings associated with your Soul. Some have been Guides and friends in other incarnations on Earth. Some of these Energy Bodies have been watching over you and others in your Soul Family since the beginning of time as you understand it. Broadly speaking, each of you has a constellation of these Energy Bodies, and you are each potentially able to achieve contact with some or all of them, depending on your level of Soul Evolution or spiritual growth. These entities are awaiting your call. Mankind is at the stage of development when it is necessary to make these connections with the Higher Self. This must take place on a grand scale before the Fourth-Dimensional shift can occur.

Now, let me go further with this explanation by discussing the concept of Soul Family. Each of you lives within what you might call your "core" family. This would be the family or families that raised you. These are the people who you call your family members. Now among this group of humans that you may or may not be related to genetically, are members of your Soul Family. These would be the Souls that have incarnated with you into your current timeframe to learn their lessons with you. These members of your Soul Family may well have participated in NUMEROUS permutations of family groupings with you throughout the millennia. Some of these family groupings may be or have been in other solar systems, on other planets and so on. For the most part, however, your Soul Family has developed in the Earthly realms. Again, members of Soul Families reincarnate together in different roles, of different sexes, of differing temperaments and so on, to experience different lessons for the Entity - the overall collective of Souls in which your Soul Family resides - and of course, for the greater experiencing of All That Is.

I must mention, that your Soul Family may include others that you may not acknowledge as "family" members. These participants might include, for example: the cashier at the local market that you may be very attracted to or perhaps find abhorrent, as well as others within your community that you hold strong emotions for. However, the Soul Family may be thought of as that small group of active participants in your reincarnational activities in your current timeframe. This primary group is the one in which you learn your lessons while other members of the group also learn their lessons.

Now if you are clever and if you learn to use your Inner Senses, you may find the connections between your current Soul Family, and the lessons learned and to be learned, as well as perhaps the most "immediate" or "recent" past lives. For those of you interested in such things, I suggest you conduct your experiments with this information in mind. The connections will then "come to mind" as you put together your Findings.

Sleep and Astral Travel

Your sleep times are highly important for your health physically, psychologically and spiritually, and so we will now comment on this state of consciousness. Now the adventures of you and your Soul Family are ongoing. Within your waking reality you experience your waking Soul Family manifestation. However, when dreaming you may be experiencing other manifestations of your Soul Family, within your current incarnation and possibly within past and future timeframes. If you watch your dreams closely, you may notice the appearance of "familiar yet unknown faces" on this inner stage of awareness. These hard-to-place characters may indeed be members of your Soul Family as they are engaged with you in activities on the subtle levels. Let me leave it at that and encourage you to do your own research in this matter.

On a biological level, as you may know, the body rests and repairs itself during sleep. Without going into too much detail, this restoration begins with the onset of sleep and continues until waking. During sleep, the consciousness, for the most part, travels from the physical body to visit locations far and wide in your Third Dimension as well as other dimensions. Your Soul, therefore, is engaged in many different activities while your physical vehicle rests and recuperates.

These sojourns from the physical body have been named Astral Travel by some of you, and this is an adequate description. You do indeed visit the Astral Levels during sleep, but there is much more to it than simply "visiting" these non-physical locales. Many purposes are served through these activities. You-the-Soul are refreshed, revitalized and energized via these inter-dimensional travels. These are the roads you have traveled for countless years while in incarnation and in the time in between lives. You know these pathways in the gridwork of the higher dimensions, as well as you know the route to take to the market in the physical world of the Third-Dimension.

Many of you are engaged in projects and collaborations on these subtle levels. Without the physical body, time takes on a fluid aspect. Travel is instantaneous. You progress by simply intending to go to a particular location. For example: you may be providing comfort to a human or group of humans who are in tragic circum-

141

stances. You may be providing support to these people in their dream state, even as you may be supported by others in yours.

As I describe in other parts of this manuscript, during sleep the consciousness also participates in the creation of what will be local, regional and worldwide waking environments. You create the framework for your reality during sleep. When you awaken, you and your fellow humans "fill in the details" by choosing from the limitless field of probable realities open to you, those that will become your Personal Reality Fields.

Extra-Terrestrials

Now without appearing sensational I would like to have a brief discussion on the phenomenon known as extra-terrestrial contact. I have spoken briefly of the extra-terrestrials in the 9/11 book and I have recently answered an inquiry from a reader on the nature of the channeled source in a popular book series in your timeframe. *(See Q&A. mf)* These volumes contain channeled messages from entities identifying themselves as figures from the Christian bible. Without naming names, I would like to say what I can on this topic without interfering in your human evolution, as I am obligated to allow those of you in the Third Dimension, to use your own free will to learn your lessons and answer your own questions without my interference. These writings I am describing, are of what you would call extra-terrestrial origins. Now, this is a misnomer. These are better described as inter-dimensional beings. And being inter-dimensional (humorously), they are far from being in outer space and beyond. They are indeed, as close to you, Dear Reader, as your most intimate physical and mental environments. They are for these reasons, quite easy to tune-in to, and many of you do just that. Let me say once again that everything in your reality has consciousness. Knowing that, how would a microbe, that has its own consciousness, intelligence and power, appear to a human, if the human tuned-in to one accidentally? One might indeed believe they had contacted a being from outer space. I will say more on this subject later in these writings.

Dialogue - Relationships between Guides
4/8/04 9:06 am

Mark - Seth what is the relationship between you and my other Guides who have identified themselves?
Seth - Yes we will have a diagram for these relationships.

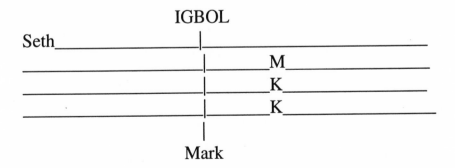

143

It will be similar to a genealogy chart, though as I have stated recently, genealogy relationships are seldom correct. Any connections between yourself and an ancestor are more a matter of chance than genetics... make that probabilities. Now to answer your question... you were asked several months ago to begin the communication with your Energy Personality, by first acting as though you had a Spirit Guide, and then when messages were forthcoming, to ask for their name. In the beginning, you received several different names. You were indeed communicating with these broader Energy Personality Entities identified as M_____, K_____, K____. Now, your Spirit Guide is a more personal matter. It would be as though an energy personality essence were "created" to the specifics of your individual personality and needs. The broader Energy Personality being the Entity from which the specific characteristics are drawn. Now beyond the Energy Personality, of course, exist continuing manifestations of energy gestalts, more complex in form and substance, until one reaches All That Is, the fundamental energy source from which all realities in all dimensions are created. Does this answer your question, somewhat?

Mark - *Yes, it gives me more clarity, for sure.*

Seth - *Let me go a bit further there... using our wonderful little metaphor of the radio dial. Suppose that you think of All That Is as the totality of all radio waves. Then on your dial you would have listed those "channeled sources" as you have so described us, on separate parts of the dial, so*

that each time you turn that dial, you connect to a different part of the energy "wavelengths" of All That Is. Now let us say at the far left of the dial is the name Seth, and when you metaphorically turn the dial to that spot, you receive through your antennae, which we might describe as the chakral receptors of the human body, the Seth transmission. And if you turn the dial to the right to the spot marked M_____, you would "pick up" the transmission of that specific Energy Body and so on. I think that our metaphor is a good one. Readers can use this visualization to tune-in to their own Guides and it becomes a ritual they can use to make these connections in their own lives. Ritualizing these activities - practicing making these connections - is what is going to help you in your Spiritual Evolution. It is the first step, Mark. Now does that answer your question?
Mark *- Yes and I really like how you've expanded the metaphor.*

The Inter-Galactic Brotherhood of Light

In my first book with my new subjects, during the course of creating material during sessions, I helped them find the connection to a group of Energy Bodies that resides within dimensions beyond your physical reality. These beings have been in contact with humanity on Earth for many, many years. They were known to your indigenous cultures for example, and they were also known to visionaries throughout the centuries in your recorded histories. They have been known by different names. Each culture that has known them, naturally, has named them through the perceptual lenses of their individual societies. This group is and has always been a very loving, gentle species of beings. Because of this loving attribute, many cultures have honored them as gods or what you might term Angels, Deities and so on. This same group I am describing is available to you for achieving contact and ongoing communications. They exist inter-dimensionally and so may provide a link to you from the distant past, in your terms, to the present and beyond. This may be said of all the Energy Bodies you may come to contact. However, the group I am describing, because they represent the evolution of peace and loving understanding within non-physical reality, may be particularly valuable advisers to you in your current reality, seeing as how you as a race are on the edge of the Fourth-Dimensional shift, with your capacity for loving understanding to be the deciding factor. This group of loving beings is called the Intergalactic Brotherhood of Light.

Dialogue - IGBOL
12/12/04 11:44 am

Mark - Seth, could you connect me to the Intergalactic Brotherhood of Light? I would like to include a conversation with them in Book II, if you agree of course.
Seth - Yes Mark, The Brotherhood will be quite pleased to speak with you. You have spoken with them on one occasion in the past, if you recall. You may wish to refer to that conversation later. Now I shall make the necessary connections

for you. You as well may need to fine-tune your receptive apparatus...

IGBOL - *You may take as long as you like to connect. We are here...*

Mark - *Who are you?*

IGBOL - *We are the IGBOL. We have spoken to you on one previous occasion personally* (in my home office. mf) *and we have spoken to your associate Cas many months ago in your office* (in my hypnotherapy office. mf).

Mark - *Can you tell me something about yourselves? For instance, what do you look like?*

IGBOL - *We are attempting to place an image of our appearance within your consciousness.* (They did indeed. mf) *As you can see, we are what you would call "of Alien extraction." You have named us. Our heads are quite larger than yours. Our eyes are much larger than yours also. We have no protruding nose formations, merely slits, as in your reptilian species. Our bodies are small and thin. Our limbs are long, our fingers thin. We are hairless. Our skin is gray in appearance. We have been called grays by some of your UFO researchers.*

Mark - *Where do you come from? Where is your home?*

IGBOL - *Our home is in a future dimension of Earth. We are you, humankind, in the progressed future.*

Mark - *How is it that you came to be "discovered" by people in our time? How do the meetings take place?*

IGBOL - *These are not accidental meetings. Our overtures to your people are part of a plan to introduce humankind to*

our civilization. We are welcoming you to the greater real-ity of which you are a part but do not recognize currently.
Mark *- You are kind then? Some of us think you mean us harm.*
IGBOL *- The opposite is true. We are beings of love. We live on love, in a very literal sense. The powerful emotion of love fuels all of reality. We know this and take advantage of love's energies. We have received negative imprinting by some of the more dangerous of your Negative Entities. Obviously, the negative beings would prefer that our kind stay out of the picture as the Nefarious Entities attempt to grasp control of your Earth in its entirety. We will not let that happen. That is why we are making ourselves known to some of you. We mean you no harm. We are providing our help to you as your people resist the takeover of your world by the Dark Forces.*
Mark *- Can you describe these Dark Forces?*
IGBOL *- Simply, consciousness creates, and as it does, both positive and what you would term "negative" creations result. Consciousness is born in love, yet love includes all manifestations of consciousness including the opposite of love. Yet because love is at the base of all realities, the tendency is to revert back to love in any given cycle. Your people in your current era are at the end of a cycle. It ap-pears to many of you that you will be consumed by negativ-ity, particularly in your U.S. However, know that Beings of Light, including our association and millions of other Light Bodies, are stemming the tide of evil. We are helping you. Yet you must do your part. You can love your way out of this*

148

dilemma. By reinforcing love within your being and in your relationships with others, you create an irresistible counterforce to the negativity in your world. The more you and your people promote love in this way, the sooner you shall subvert the agenda of the Negative Entities. Our wish for you is to realize that we are with you in support of your loving evolution as a race. We are not the enemy. We have been slandered by the Negative Entities. Look for our appearance on the world stage as we all - meaning humanity as well as the Light Bodies - unite to overturn the evil ones. That is all. 12:12 pm (Coincidentally, it's 12:12 on 12/12/04! mf)

Experiment - Contacting the Intergalactic Brotherhood of Light
Hypothesis: the igbol are the "closest" and most accessible of the light bodies

Now, you can be informed of which being or group of beings you are allied with by virtue of your evolution as a Soul. This can be discovered by asking your Energy Personality, using your free will to ask the names and locations of other beings associated with You-the-Soul. The IGBOL is the "closest" to you in terms of affinity of purpose. They are on a path of loving understanding as are you the reader. This is why we have suggested that you contact this group as a preliminary to further explorations. Let me say that you need not fear approaching this group in your experiments. As I state often in this book, the great majority of you are in all probability, members of The Seth Entity and so have a direct connection to these Energy Bodies we are describing. The Seth Entity is vast, again as I have noted previously, and at this time we are having a "reunion" of sorts on these subtle levels. You may assume you are rekindling old relationships in these communications, for indeed you are. The fear and mistrust will fade as you receive memories of these associations, in the form of divine impulses. Since it is I Seth who is writing this book, you may be assured that I will do what I can to assist you in establishing contact with these loving Energy Bodies and guiding you on your individual path of Soul Evolution. You will know it when you feel it. This is ongoing assistance I am providing as a Being of Light in service to mankind during this time of awakening.

Perform Your Ritual of Sanctuary

Establish your relaxed state of consciousness. Now with the assurance and confidence that comes with mastering these various levels of consciousness through the experiments done in the preceding chapters, have the intention and profound expectation that you will encounter these loving beings. The contact comes with attendant feelings of compassion and love. There may be an "alien" component that may cause discomfort. You may go beyond surface appearances by utilizing your skills at turning fear and anger into loving understanding and confidence. The IGBOL are you, Dear Reader, in your multidimensional future. Knowing this, you may experience this contact as a homecoming. When you sense that the meeting is over, gradually come back to your Third-Dimensional awareness.

Findings - Document your experiences in contacting the IGBOL.

Experiment - Becoming aware of Astral Travel during sleep.

Hypothesis: you can use your intention to become aware of astral travel during sleep

Perform Your Ritual of Sanctuary

The Ritual of Sanctuary is important here in this investigation. Perform it just as you are falling asleep, with suggestions to yourself that you will become aware of your inner environment - your sleeping world - as you are about to engage in Astral Travel as you call it. It may be necessary to conduct this experiment for several days to get results. The suggestion that you will become aware within the dream state is important. You may also suggest that you will awaken after a particular sojourn into the Astral Realms, so that you may document your experiences in your dream journal or other medium. It would then be advantageous to return to sleep with the suggestion that you will awaken briefly to document your further Astral Travels, and so on. This will give you an ongoing record of your adventures during sleep. And again, the more experience you gain though experimentation in the dream state, the greater mastery gained in perceiving and documenting this state of awareness. **Findings** - Document your findings, perhaps with a journal or tape recorder.

CHAPTER EIGHT

You Are the Vanguard

Dialogue - Being Exposed
1/21/04 5:15 pm

Mark - Can you comment on my fears that people who have authority over me will punish me if they see my picture in the paper talking about you?

Seth - Well Mark, you know well where your fears in this matter originate. Think for a moment. This is your greatest concern since you were a child - being found out for what you believe, what you may be ashamed of. You are on the path continuing from your childhood research into the unexplained phenomena of your Earth. Could there ever be a better time to "come clean" on these lifelong pursuits? When you do you may feel the liberation that comes with expressing who you really are - to your family, to your friends, to the vast public if you will. All that you are losing are your fears and your limitations.

Giving Up Power

You are not guilty. You are not to blame. You, Dear Reader, have done nothing wrong. Because you are in the habit of giving away your power to others, you leave yourself in a vulnerable position. You relinquish your power and then the usurper of your power - parent, employer, priest, politician - can use guilt and other unsavory emotional states to control you. Yet you have done nothing wrong. You only think you have, second-to-second, because of this manipulation by those in perceived authority. They want you to feel guilty and powerless. It makes their job much easier when you are afraid, anxious, experiencing feelings of low self-worth etc. etc. etc. How much easier it is to take money from someone, for example, when they are feeling unworthy. Indeed, after you have ceded your power to people and institutions, no wonder you feel unworthy. Yet again, you are not guilty of a thing. You are not to blame. Now, that is not to say that you are absolved of all responsibility in the matters of power between yourself and those in your world. That is not what I am suggesting at all. For that matter, the main reason I have returned to resume my communications with those of you on your great Earth at this time, is to help you get your power back. We cannot have a revolution in human consciousness with so many humans without the full human power that they were incarnated with when entering into life on your world.

Currently in your timeframe there is much talk of "taking back power" - personal empowerment. It is almost a cliche in your world. Yet truly taking back your power from persons and institutions is a heroic act. There is much perceived risk in doing so, for most Western humans fear reprisals when they go beyond the status quo. There may be feelings of guilt that come with "not doing what you are told."

You also may have feelings of loneliness. Breaking away from the pack may leave you feeling as though you have made a mistake in surrendering the safety of the group. Yet also know that as more of you go on your Soul journeys, relinquishing the negatives in your lives, pursuing positive, loving experiences and creating a radically different world for yourselves, you will also meet up with others who are on a similar path. Those with positive loving thoughts will be drawn to others who have positive loving thoughts. As you meet with others on a similar path, you will form groups, naturally as humans do, and soon you will have remade your social institutions into something truly sacred and life-affirming for all.

You Are the Vanguard

The notion that you are going too far with this exploration of consciousness, that you are going into "forbidden" territory where few have gone before you, may cause you to become fearful, wishing you had not begun the journey. This is a natural reaction, and I wholly expect many of you, especially those with religious conditioning, to at first react with fear and anxiety when you "see something in the dark."

First, this IS forbidden territory you are exploring. Your religions tell you that you need an intermediary, a priest, to communicate with the deities and those on "the other side." This conditioning can be difficult to undo for some of you. But again, I urge you to persevere. The benefit will be a freedom that you have in all probability not experienced in your lifetime.

The reasons that few have gone before you to explore this side of human consciousness, are that they were, of course, prevented from doing so by the priests and various other intermediaries in the religious hierarchies, and also because the great majority of humans are conditioned to not question the where, what and whys of their own lives. For example: how many of you reading this book will talk about your experiences to your parents, or to your friends and relatives or to your business associates? Now whether you do share this information with them will naturally depend on how open your relationships are with them. But on the whole, I would guess that the majority of you will keep your investigations and findings to yourselves, not only because this is a private spiritual matter, but because you may be afraid of being called a witch or other "emotionally loaded" descriptive term.

Yet understand, there is no benefit in creating these connections with your Higher Self in an environment of fear, as if you were doing something "naughty." Fortunately, in all likelihood, the undercurrent of love and compassion you will experience as you are guided into these new lands, will give you the courage to tell others about your findings. Naturally, I would suggest you are reasonably certain they will take your messages to heart with an open mind. There is no benefit in talking to the authorities, for instance, about your incredible journeys, when you know they may not share your zeal of discovery (humorously).

You are the Vanguard, my friend. There was a reason for your picking up this book and reading it. This may mark the acknowledgment to yourself that you are on your path. In a way, it is similar to making an appointment and keeping it. Yet here, the appointment may have been made in previous lifetimes or in the time before incarnations. You will receive information on where and when these decisions were made, if you simply ask yourself, now in this moment. Everything becomes a meaningful experience. Every action is a coincidence. When you acknowledge that you are on your path of Soul Evolution, each moment in physical reality becomes an opportunity for spiritual growth and Value Fulfillment.

Dialogue - Troubled Friend
4/14/04 9:20 am

Mark - *It looks to me like my friend does not take responsibility for their creations. They blame everyone but themselves for their difficulties.*
Seth - *Mark, be ruthlessly loving in this matter. Prove yourself an adequate match for this person in this endeavor by*

reflecting back love and faith and confidence when they test you out of fear and mistrust. The trick is to identify the incoming negative Consciousness Units and transform them with your energy into loving thoughts and emotions BEFORE they enter your energy field and cause disruptions. These energies are very powerful. They are indeed like parasites that attach themselves to your Energy Body where they then can attach themselves to others, but only if the host is fearful, mistrusting and negative and only if the target is also fearful, mistrusting, cynical etc. Negativity is the feeding ground for these energies. Where there is only love and acceptance and compassion, these influences cannot take hold.

Mark - *I'm thinking that your point is about personal responsibility. We have to individually take responsibility for our thoughts and actions. It makes sense, because integrity seems to flow from this.*

Seth - *Mark, integrity is an excellent concept and we can discuss it a bit here. In this situation, you are integrating your Soul aspects of loving kindness and acceptance, with your core personality or egoic aspects of self-defense, anger etc. So integrate, integrate, integrate (humorously). Love dissolves the egoic responses motivated by territoriality and competition. Coming together - integration - is what is needed here on all levels. Common ground, conciliation, cooperation for a higher ideal, these are all relevant issues to be considered at this time. Now Mark, know that many of your contemporaries are also involved in these Soul is-*

sues. Your planet is going through a transformation that will be felt down through every atom in your perceptive field. All is in flux. Everyone's issues are being presented to them for transformation and healing. Now you can ignore these "requests" from Soul, but you do so at your peril. These lessons will help you gain the wisdom and skills necessary to make the transition into the Unity of Consciousness Dimension and stay there. The more deeply this divine information is taken into your being, the more likely you will retain it, remember it and use it in your spiritual pursuits.

(Later I received a "memo" from Seth - the Negative Entities are created by negative thoughts and emotions, but it is unproductive to ask which came first, the Negative Entities or the ideas and emotions that created them, for all exists at once. The hope lies in more people opting for courage and love rather than fear and anger. mf)

Your Single Loving Thought

Perhaps some of the readers of this book, considering the constant perceived negativity surrounding you, wonder how one person could possibly make a difference in the global picture. You may be asking yourselves, 'Why should I go through the effort of changing my beliefs and my Personal Reality for the better, if it will be only a "drop in the bucket" in the greater scheme of things?" My answer to you would be that your efforts in changing your beliefs and behaviors and thus your Personal Reality Fields, also have the added effects of broadcasting by example, the benefits of loving kindness and confidence to those around you in your physical reality. The effects are also felt telepathically. As you change your personal world for the better, you are each moment broadcasting on the subtle levels your successes in overcoming negativity to the collective network of Souls on your planet in your timeframe. You are linked to every other Soul on your planet through this web of subtle energies. I have noted elsewhere in these writings that you as a species are literally "One." You are all co-creating with All That Is your individual lives, yet you are all sharing the same timeframe as One People. This Telepathic Network is your communication system that you use to achieve consensus while sleeping, on what will be manifested as your world reality upon awakening. So you see, YOU can truly make a difference. Thoughts have power. Thoughts of good intent and loving kindness have extreme transformative power. Your positive thoughts seek out other positive images and thoughts being transmitted in this collective mental conversation. These thoughts merge to create incipient Reality Constructs. When these potentialities reach a stage of imminent creation, it could be YOUR SINGLE LOVING THOUGHT that could tip the scales towards the positive manifestation.

This mental conversation does indeed continue while you are awake and going about your activities. In other words, you are still dreaming and in contact with the collective while awake, but it goes on "in the background." It is just as important to create the thoughts of loving kindness and confidence while awake, because that is when you have the most conscious control over your mentality. It is this exercise of consciously changing your thoughts and behaviors that creates a spillover into your dream world, your sleeping times, affecting the world thought consensus in a positive way.

Now you may still be harboring the belief that "evil," particularly in your times, may be stronger than "good." Indeed, with the variety of wars, famines and other negative events going on around you, this would seem to be the case. However, this belief is still only a habitual idea that you hold. You may have been in the habit of thinking to yourself, "Evil triumphs over good: in politics, in business, in my personal dealings with people," that you have blinded yourself to other options, other ways of perceiving your world. Look beyond these perceptual blinders and you may see that the opposite is true: Good triumphs over evil: in politics, in business, in your personal dealings with people. The opposite is true my friend. Reflect on this for a moment and see if you agree.

Effects of Terrorism

Terrorism is our theme for this communique from The Seth Entity. In your world, terrorism is the subject of choice for modern humans. You are enthralled with the subject for you are daily inundated with terrorist data from the various negative media to the degree that many of you in the modern world eat, drink and sleep terror.

As I covered in the 9/11 manuscript, you "like" it that way, for you have become entranced by your negative leaders and the negative media into believing that these terrorist issues should occupy your every waking hour. Your leaders like it that way, for that is the way they want you to respond. The negative leaders are in the business of control, and so in a way they use their proclamations to control you through fear. The fear produces body chemicals that create stress and anxiety as well as addiction to these fear-producing statements. You just can't take your eyes off it. You just can't ignore the headlines. And so the negative media like it that way, for they are profiting tremendously by spreading the negative messages of the negative leaders.

Now, I must remind you of a lifesaving point here: you create your own reality. At the risk of repeating myself, let us visit that concept again. On an individual and collective basis, humans create their individual Reality Fields and the mass-created consensus reality that you perceive in a linear fashion. Let us use an example to see how the negative leaders and their media "help" you form your individual and also your mass consciousness realities. It's quite simple really... You are an average American who awakens to the sound of the radio news program that describes the latest atrocity perpetrated by the latest enemy of your country. Can you see how this sets the tone for the remainder of your day? Before becoming fully awake, in that "in between state" in which you are so impressionable, your mind is already picking up negative information that you will, no doubt, carry with you throughout the day. And as your mind finds in your mental and physical environments what it feels is "corroboration" of this negative information - proof - it will note this proof and add it to the mix of negative data, beliefs, images and so on.

Again, in this way, the negative leaders and the negative media have won the contest for control of the minds of individual listeners and viewers and also have they gained control of the <u>masses</u> of listeners and viewers. Now, since telepathy among humans is operative continually, you reinforce this negativity on the subtle levels by communicating with other humans in the collective, on the negative ideas and images presented to you by the negative leaders and their media. On these subtle levels ideas are accepted as fact, though there may have been NO CRITICAL THINKING involved in accessing this data. Do you see how your leaders, your media and your unaware selves conspire to terrorize you? You are terrorizing yourselves. It is true that your leaders are at most fault for your predicament. But you as human individuals are also responsible for your dilemma. You have not taken individual responsibility for your own thoughts and actions. You have given your power to institutions, to leaders, to employers. No wonder then do you find yourselves afraid and powerless.

Obviously, the most direct and simple way to take your power back from the institutions of global negative media would be to not participate in them. As I have suggested at different stages in this new material, you can always TURN OFF THE RADIO, TURN OFF THE TV, TURN OFF THE VIOLENT MOVIES. Avoid the negative media when you are out in your physical environment. Vote with your pocketbook by not purchasing negative, violent, controlling media and other life-denying products of your mass-consumption society. You will soon begin to like it - your freedom - and your negative institutions and leaders will begin to not like it. The repression may grow then, because "the powers that be" will know that you are taking responsibility for your own thoughts and beliefs. However, persevere and your numbers will surely grow. The Forces of Light are in your favor. The probabilities for a mass transformation of consciousness into the positive arena are growing. Your contribution is necessary for the greater good of your species and your Mother Earth.

The Negative Leaders

This next section concerns a critical issue with regards to the actions of your leaders in the U.S. and some of the other developed nations. The actions of these countries, particularly in the Middle East, where they seek to control the oil, are challenging the basic structure of acceptable behavior on your planet. Now there are those in my dimension who take notice of such things and we are quite concerned with the zeal with which these deluded humans continue to plunder your beloved Earth. Certainly many of my readers may wonder what they can do personally about this critical matter, that of the brutality and warlike nature of your leaders, and I presented some exercises in the 9/11 book to answer these questions. However, some time has lapsed since that material was created and conditions have greatly worsened as of the time of this writing. I feel that I, as a protector of your planet, must look for more effective methods to counter the negative leaders. Now I know some of you may scoff and say, "What can you do, as a non-physical entity, to effect change on this Earth?" The truth is that Beings of Light such as myself have exercised our power, in what you would call your "history," in concerted efforts to effect quite dramatic changes in your Earth reality. These changes were brought about by our efforts in tandem with the mental and physical efforts of human beings. Each of you, as I have stated earlier, has an Energy Personality or Spirit Guide if you wish, that has watched over you from your birth into your current lifetime. Whether you acknowledge this as true or not does not in any way deny the truth of my statement.

Now consider what could be accomplished for the good of humankind, if many thousands, hundreds of thousands, millions of human beings were to act in unison toward a common goal, such as for instance, the creation of peace on your world, peace in the Middle East and all of the other areas of conflict on your world. How would we accomplish this, as peacemakers, you and I and your loving Guides? As with all in creation, you do it with your thoughts. First you acknowledge that you have an Energy Personality. You affirm this, have the intention of communicating with it, and then experience the unfolding of that relationship in the manifestation. I covered this earlier in the book, but I would like now to suggest an experiment on a grand scale. First let me repeat one of the basic elements of my teaching: you are not separate from anything in the Universe. You, Dear Reader, are at the center of the Universe, and you are connected to everything in it by virtue of your thoughts. If you believe this, or you can make the attempt to believe this, it follows that Peace on Earth is well within your grasp.

What if the soldier refused to fight? What if the soldier had a dream one evening that so affected him that he refused to fight? What if your negative media propagators had a change of heart and decided to state the truth instead of lies and propaganda? What if hundreds of thousands of people awakened one morning to discover that they had a change of heart and would no longer support the negative leaders? I think you may be getting my point here. When you go into your meditations and you direct your energies, instead of sending out the positive images and emotions to just one or two, send out the energies to the Guides and to their physical counterparts throughout all of humanity. Your thoughts have power. Indeed your thoughts are the most powerful elements in your physical reality, for THEY CREATE YOUR PHYSICAL REALITY. If you desire peace on your Earth, then use your powerful thoughts to create it.

Link up with other peace lovers on the subtle levels and imagine your peaceful world into being.

Dialogue - The Seth Reunion
6/8/04 11:29 am

Mark - Seth, any dictation? I have 30 minutes.
Seth - Good morning Mark. Are you feeling less stressed since you put in your ad in the paper?
Mark -Yes.
Seth - Now you have committed yourself and now you have begun the manifestation in earnest. You are creating it now, Mark. The fear has dissolved. Perhaps some related dictation... fear in this moment remembers perceived "past" fear, mistakes and guilt, and so manifests from these negative emotional templates, the perceived negative future, and reinforces the perceived negative "past." Confidence and love in this moment remembers perceived "past" confidence, victories and joy, and so manifests from these positive templates, the positive future.
Mark - Thanks Seth. That is useful information.

Experiment - Other Lives in the Vanguard
(Magician Shaman Witch Healer)
Hypothesis: current interests may illustrate other lives in the vanguard

If you are an avid reader of my material, new or old, you are in all likelihood simply reaffirming in this current existence, predilections of interest and behavior from other Simultaneous Lives. The members of The Seth Entity are not, for the most part, stay-at-home bodies, who allow the world to go by them unchanged, unnoticed. No, my fellow travelers are eager to question the core values and beliefs of their cultures. Yet this questioning is not entirely intellectual, it is backed-up with advocacy and action in the physical domain. This action has behind it the spiritual impetus for transformation for the good of all. You are a very humanitarian group and you make your marks on your culture in very noticeable ways.

You will be protected. As you exercise your power to create loving realities, you will be protected by Beings of Light. You have the collective power of goodness on your side, you see, and so as you go about your activist duties in response to the inner promptings of divine information, you may notice that the way before you is cleared of barriers to your destination. As in my earlier example of the "crystal people," you may have incarnated many times in many eras, but with a single emphasis or role: that of advocate for humanity. And so you may notice that you respond to threats upon others as threats upon yourself. You take the threats upon your fellow Earthly inhabitants and upon the Earth in very personal ways. On this note, let us explore possible lives lived just as you may now be living this current life of yours, as an advocate for humanity and for your Mother Earth.

Now you may have lived lives as Empowered Ones within "normal" occupations that no one would suspect. This may be true for you currently, Dear Reader. Many of you use your nondescript careers - housewife, teacher, mason - to protect your true identities - magician, shaman, witch, healer. The true calling is protected. There is a tradition in these matters to work "undercover," and avoid the scrutiny that comes with self-disclosure. Naturally, it is always your choice to reveal or to not reveal your true motives and the real work that you are accomplishing. But as I have just stated: you will be protected. As a bringer of light and healing, you will be protected from harm.

Perform your Ritual of Sanctuary

The previous experiments in this book in contacting Simultaneous Lives lived in other timeframes may well have given you glimpses into lives lived as Empowered Ones. There is a certain unifying aspect among all of your reincarnational existences, and it may well be that you have come into physical reality on these various occasions to help and to heal. With your Energy Personality as your guide, imagine other lives in other eras in which you may have served in the Vanguard of progressive human consciousness.

Findings - Document your findings in your preferred way.

Experiment - Responding to Negative Realities.
Hypothesis: you can superimpose positive realities over negative realities

Perform your Ritual of Sanctuary

Please think of a time from your past when you felt that you were living life to its fullest and you were amazed at yourself for your accomplishments. Now the primary objective here is to recreate the feelings of self-worth and confidence you felt during this experience or time in your life. The second phase in this experiment is to amplify these positive feelings. Imagine for yourself a dial or a switch that enables you to strengthen these positive feelings just by turning the dial or flipping the switch. Now dial or flip the switch and experience the strengthening of positive feelings of accomplishment and self-worth. You will experience differing levels of emotion depending on your life experiences and personality aspects. However, all of you will in all probability experience an increase in positive feelings. Try adjusting the dial and working with the features of your switch to further increase positive feelings and emotions. Do this experiment for a few minutes per day with the objective that you will be able to gradually increase your control over your emotional states. Once you have gained some experience in controlling your emotional states, you may experiment in superimposing your positive reality directly over the negative reality you are experiencing. When you are successful, you will notice a dramatic shift to the positive within your Personal Reality Field.

Now these experiments are vital for you as a way to learn emotional control. In the Fourth Dimension, emotional control will enable you to keep your focus in the mental aspects of consciousness. You will not be dragged back into the emotional reactivity of the Third Dimension.

Findings - Document your findings.

CHAPTER NINE

The Fourth-Dimensional Shift

Dialogue - The Seth Reunion
6/26/04 8:58 am

Mark - Well Seth, your Reunion Party is tonight. Do you have anything to say to me beforehand?

Seth - Yes Mark. Congratulations, the manifestation for prosperity and happiness is unfolding for your perception. You are embarking upon the world tour. You will be assisting your audiences to engage the Energy Personality and begin the exploration of Fourth-Dimensional reality. Let that be your main point when you speak. Now, with regards to the media: this is a spiritual practice similar to others, and so it would be good to draw that as a baseline for discussion. Some will attempt to draw you into discussions of the old material, the validity of the current material etc. Diversions. It will be simple for you to keep on the message that this is entirely new information from a different personality essence of The Seth Entity. Seth has personalized and customized his expression to meet the needs of this current collaboration with Mark, his Third Subject. You can tell them just that. Think of every contact at the party and in the field as a media contact. For as I said before, the material will be popularized via word of mouth, as readers speak with their friends and families. The _____ website is indeed a good model for you to follow. _____ is a well-respected Entity in my domain. This Entity is gentle and knowledgeable. Feel free to promote our service in the way that _____ and the _____ team have promoted their work. Tonight, simply ask for me to come through when you wish. I will come in strong enough so that you can simply rest, and allow me to run the show, if you wish.

Mark *- I do wish that. But of course, please don't give out any embarrassing or personal information about us.*

Seth *- Of course not Mark. I will be utterly discreet and charming (humorously).*

Mark *- Thanks Seth.*

Prophesies

The idea of a dimensional shift is not new to humankind. Many of your world's religions foretell similar events in their prophecies. Different words and concepts are used to explain the coming shift, but in fact, we may all be describing the same thing, with a different emphasis on particular points. Indeed, the breakthrough into higher dimensions is at the base of virtually all of your Earth's spiritual systems. Certainly you the reader can confirm this statement for yourself. Simply replace the words "Fourth Dimension" with "Heaven" or any other term from any culture on your world denoting the Etheric Plane. And again, these portals to the higher dimensions open to humankind very infrequently. The coming shift, for instance, will occur at the end of a many-thousands-of-years cycle. It has been foretold in the scriptures of indigenous peoples, such as the Mayan and Hopi. The symbolism depicted in these prophecies, I might add, is a great deal more accurate than some of the Christian stories. Yet, as I said, we may be all describing the same event, merely with a particular cultural emphasis on dates, related gods and goddesses, and so on.

Now the world over, as we create this manuscript, all of humankind is being readied for this event. Other Light Bodies conversant in the cultures assigned to them, are bringing their collectives of humans into a witnessing of the precursor events that will herald the Fourth-Dimensional Shift. You know by now what I am speaking about, if you are paying attention at all to my words (humorously). The Earth Changes - floods, hurricanes, tornadoes, glacier melting - are the heralds to the shift. The turmoil of human thought is creating these changes. In a way, you as a race are setting yourselves up for a very positive or very negative experience here with this shift. There is always the probability that you will allow conditions to deteriorate to such a degree that there will be no turning back and you will destroy yourselves with your own negative thoughts. However, humans are quite fond of saving themselves from the brink of disaster, as is also documented in many of your spiritual scripts. Whatever the outcome, know that we are watching you and will intercede if and when we can. Again, the Laws of Non-Interference prohibit certain types of intervention. These messages I am conveying to you through my human counterparts are of a benign and subtle type of intervention. Dramatic "rescuing efforts" are obviously not allowed. You must learn your lessons as a race and as individuals.

When you learn how to access your Energy Personality and other Guides, you will experience firsthand what I am describing to you. When you are experiencing the free flow of divine information into your consciousness, you will eventually dispense with the need for continually challenging the divine source as to veracity and specifics. You will no longer require proof, for you will be LIVING your proof. You will no longer require prophecy, for you will be LIVING the prophecy. These dramatic transformations are already underway for you the reader of this book, and to some degree for every other human on your planet. The spiritual revolution of human and Earthly consciousness has begun. The Soul Self is making itself known. As this manifestation develops, visionaries from all spheres of activity on your world will step into leadership roles. Now you might ask, "Will they be elected into these roles?" I would answer, "Not necessarily." They will, for the most part, "assume" these roles. In the West, as I have mentioned before, your political processes will soon be rendered obsolete, as the citizens of Earth take back the power to govern themselves.

Mother Nature

These transformations in human consciousness and thus the Third-Dimensional physical reality we are discussing, have been noted in your media. "Strange" weather patterns and Earth Changes are now commonplace around the world and the media report these unusual events. Often these stories are couched in terms of your Mother Nature displaying her power: power to upset the plans of humans to go to their sporting events, to the beaches for relaxation, to their weddings and other outdoor events. In an almost whimsical fashion these news stories often personify these weather changes as due to your Mother Nature's unpredictability, but in a lighthearted way. Yet the more potent and destructive events are described as something to be feared. In these instances, Mother Nature has become so unpredictable, no one knows when she will reveal her "anger" and strike you with a bolt of lightening, or rise a flood to carry you away in your automobile or cause an earthquake to bring down your great cities. Now, if you have read my books, you have been acquainted with the truth about the weather and about all physical manifestations. All physical reality in your dimension is the result of attendant thoughts and beliefs your humankind hold in the mass consciousness.

Let me go further… you have a saying in the West that "everyone talks about the weather but no one does anything about it." In fact, this is not true. Each person on your planet has "a say" in how the weather will be expressed in their area at any given moment. This individual contribution is done, for the most part, under your awareness. The Consciousness Units, through the individual expression of emotion, combine with other Consciousness Unit expressions of emotional content from the population of any given area. These streams of incipient Reality Constructs combine and are expressed in the manifestation of particular weather patterns and Earth Changes according to how the influences play out within the collective consciousness of that region of the world. Now I must mention that when I say "mass consciousness of a particular region," I include the collective "thoughts, ideas and mentality" of everything in that region, including the rocks, the soil, the trees and the created products for mass consumption. All has consciousness and all contribute to physical manifestations of weather and Earth Changes. Now, obviously a bug might have less of an effect upon the weather than an angry, fearful human (humorously), but the bug does indeed contribute in measurable ways to the collective manifestation.

So do you see how many of you simply project your fears upon this great entity, your Mother Earth, forsaking your own responsibility in the creation of your physical reality? It was not always thus, however. In fact, in civilizations from your past, the weather was created quite consciously to support adequate conditions for the growth of particular crops, for outside celebrations and for other purposes. This takes place even today in some of your aboriginal cultures on your planet. Your modern scientists, also, are in a race to develop technologies to change the weather for profit, for the profit of corporations to which they are beholden. This matter will be discussed in future volumes. For now, let us explore, as Scientists of Consciousness, the Home Dimension of friends and family.

Experiment - Tuning-In to Friends and Family in their Home Dimension
Hypothesis: the dearly departed await your contact

Conduct your Ritual of Sanctuary

Now, this is an experiment in contacting your friends or family members in their Home Dimension. Obviously, if you are still too upset to attempt this contact, please do not consider trying this experiment. For some of you it may be best experienced after you have gained some emotional distance from the event of The Transition. Find a comfortable chair to sit in or perhaps a comfortable sofa or bed. The idea is to relax the body enough so that you can receive these impulses from the other side, yet not so relaxed that you fall asleep. In between worlds is where you want to be for this experiment and so I ask you to make those preparations you need to in order to enter that state. Now the crux of this experiment is to distinguish, from the chorus of telepathic messages you are receiving in your relaxed state, those messages that are being transmitted by your loved ones. Beings of Light, friends and loved ones and other Entities from your past, present and future, are all constantly vying for your attention in this mental environment. Since you are attempting to focus your Inner Senses, you might simply visualize the appearance of the loved-one. Mentally picture your family member or friend as though they were speaking to you just as they would when they were in the physical body. Fill the perception with color and enliven it with your thoughts. This will have the effect of your "tuning-in" to their communication band, allowing you to "home-in" on them, in a manner of speaking. Now it is important to proceed with this experiment as a loving Scientist of Consciousness. Love and kindness are your watchwords in these endeavors. Ego perceptions have no place here.

As you create the image of the person in your mental environment, imagine their voice becoming gradually stronger and stronger until it becomes the most prominent voice in your inner chorus. Use your intention and simply turn up the volume or use the metaphor of the radio dial to do so. This is very easy to do and I am certain you will find success with this in a short period of time. After establishing contact - you will know you have contact if you feel the intense loving vibrations that emanate from the Home Dimension - simply have your conversation, just as you did when your loved-one was in physical reality. After the conversation, naturally say good-bye and perhaps make an appointment to speak again in the future.

Then use your metaphor of the radio dial or which-
ever technique you used to make contact, to release
contact with your loved-one. Gradually come back to
your waking consciousness. In time, if you give yourself the suggestions and if you have the ongoing intention to do so for loving purposes, you will be able
to make these contacts with the departed while you
are at work, walking in the park, etc. etc. etc. As you
use the Inner Senses, they strengthen over time.

Findings - Immediately document your personalized
findings.

CHAPTER TEN

A New World

Dialogue - Core Beliefs
4/7/04 5:04 pm

Mark - Seth, can you comment on our recent business dealings with your first book? Is this the beginning of the "prosperity sequence" you've spoken of recently?

Seth - Mark, you are in the middle of your "prosperity sequence," you just do not realize it. All time in your dimension is simultaneous. You just have to experience events sequentially to understand them. It would be confusing for you, would it not, to see a cake being cooked in one of your ovens, rise and complete its cooking in seconds, rather than minutes? So you manifest according to rules "built into" your reality. Fortunately you all "obey" the same rules - telepathy is operative on all levels - otherwise you would all be confused at the unpredictability of your world. Now, our work represents some tinkering with these built-in rules and regulations, these core beliefs. In my manuscripts of long ago, I spoke of the difficulty in changing these core assumptions. Now is a different era, my friend, and you and your fellow Earthly associates are being prepared to change the core beliefs that you hold. This preparation is taking place during your dream state. Most of you do not realize this is happening. You simply awaken with more clarity and a feeling that anything is possible for you: this despite the wars and the famine and other negative phenomena so evident around you.

You Are Already There

A new world is coming and yet you are already there. As you read this second book of mine, divine information is being streamed into your Energy Body. This information is your heritage. It is the truth regarding your circumstances as a living Entity on your Earth. This truth is simple. It can be stated in just a few words: you are ageless; you never die. The Soul Self that is at your core is eternal and has witnessed countless seasons on your Earth and on other planets and in other galaxies and dimensions.

And you, my friend, you and I are one. We are all one and it has always been that way. When I speak of our connections to each other I am speaking of literal energy networks that tie each conscious cell to every other conscious cell in all of created reality. It is through this network that All That Is, the ultimate energy source, seeks to know itself through your experiences. Now, you have a physical body and so the truth of this fact may be somewhat difficult to experience. However, do not wait until your death to receive this information. Take advantage of these teachings I offer you in this life. This is the ultimate simple test for you in physical reality: will you take up the challenge to learn your lessons now, or will you postpone your awakening until the time of your physical death or in other lifetimes? The choice is always yours. But do not wait until it is too late. You may be required to incarnate on your negative Earth another time, to be again given a chance to learn your lessons.

Spirituality

Yes, spirituality, as you may be coming to an understanding of this phenomenon, is simply the experiencing of Earthly existence by your embodied Soul. There need be no religious connotations. Thoughtforms that reflect memories, recent and ancient, of genocide perpetrated by religious movements, do not <u>necessarily</u> have a place in this discussion of what we are calling "spirituality." So you see, there is a practical approach to our studies of Third-Dimensional reality. You are undergoing a restoration, if you will, to your original, self-comprehending, godlike awareness. You are all Avatars. You know this on a certain level and as you awaken, your knowing shall "firm up" and become a great deal more supportive for you as you transform your beliefs and ideas about what is possible. Spirituality is a remembrance of what it has been for you in ages past. This is true. Yet it also points the way for you into the future when you shall be called upon to remake your social and political and SPIRITUAL institutions. Therefore, I caution you and yours in using your cynicism and distrust to keep your spiritual transformation at bay. Rather, I suggest you embrace it. Go with the flow.

May I remind you that for every moment of your perceived reality, your waking reality, is a complementary moment in one or more of your Simultaneous Lives? So each moment of spiritual unfolding bears the mark of all simultaneously-experienced moments in your multiple reincarnational lives. Now there are, of course, differences in the various aspects of your simultaneously-lived lives, for they are all being lived, for the most part, in different eras, by different sexes and nationalities etc, for the greater learning of All That Is. But please understand, quite literally, when you may be experiencing a moment of ecstatic understanding here in you current Moment Point in this timeframe, one or perhaps many more of your Simultaneous Lives may be experiencing a timeless moment also, but as I said, most definitely, within a different physical body, of a different emotional makeup and station in Soul Evolution than you, Dear Reader of this book. I want you to ponder the enormity of this fact of life, for just a moment (humorously).

Now because my friend Mark here is signaling to me telepathically that I should be more forthcoming with this divine information, I shall "give up more data," as you say... When you meet a friend on the street, unexpectedly, perhaps a friend you have not seen for some time, you may be ecstatic, overjoyed, as you embrace and speak of your relationship, how good it is to see that person again after so long etc. Now in that moment of reunion, that spacious moment of reunion, you are also, in another body, in another era, most probably on your Earth, experiencing a complementary type of reunion activity. Further, if you could take a motion picture or snapshot of the various reunion activities of your various lives during that moment, you would find that there are also NUMEROUS correlations between these experiences. You may find on observing these movies or pictures that the settings - streets, fields, within structures - are quite similar, in that the placement of objects, trees, rocks, houses or what have you - are similar throughout. Is it not obvious that your experiences we are describing here, the reunion experiences, are all quite similar, because you are the multi-dimensional creator of these events? As the creator of worlds here, most naturally, your creations would bear the mark of the maker - the creator who is indeed you, in tandem with All That Is. So now as you observe your moment-to-moment experiences, remember that this is only the "surface" of a deeper experience of manifestation that is your multi-dimensional being.

Seth Lecture Series

For the interested reader, Mark is at the time of this writing, planning a lecture tour. He is putting his faith in me to channel the appropriate material while he is in front of the paying public. As you may know, I have not spoken in a public way for well over twenty years. I was never that enamored of public mediumship while working with my First and Second Subjects. However, my Third Subject possesses the skills and the desire to bring my messages directly to you. Our purposes in this endeavor are to present this new material to as many people as possible in a direct, one-on-one fashion, hoping to catalyze within individuals, the beginning of the great adventure of humankind in your time-frame - the quest for connection with the Energy Personality and the exploration of the Unity of Consciousness Dimension. Now, you may receive this catalyst through the written word, the printed word as in books. Your energy centers or "chakras" as you call them, can be opened by reading my material. This is probably the simplest way for you to commence with the work at hand. However, for those of you who feel you may be called for a more direct experience, you may attend the lectures and affirm your connection to The Seth Entity in this way. In these direct interfaces with lecture attendees, much more divine information can be transmitted and absorbed in a very brief time, compared to the reading of books, solitary meditations and so on.

Now we are also working on a means of connecting to interested parties through other media, such as the Internet and recorded materials. Again, "the window of opportunity" for humans to engage the Soul Self and grow spiritually, is becoming smaller with each passing month. The culmination of countless years of evolution will soon be at hand.

This activity is not something that can be postponed until you "have the time" to address the issue. You are virtually OUT OF TIME at this time (humorously). Your suspicions that time seems to be speeding up are quite pointedly true. You are, as a race, speeding toward the great transformation, and indeed, the short time that remains ahead of you will be perceived as a VERY short time, particularly if you have procrastinated and avoided your responsibilities regarding your Soul Issues: the deeply personal lessons you have come to your Earthly existence to learn.

I urge you to participate in your spiritual practices, in your churches and religions if they serve You-the-Soul, in your readings of the great Masters and in your seeking direct contact with disseminators of my messages and the messages of other Light Bodies. Now, the negative energy forms, the Negative Entities, will be attempting to discourage you from walking your spiritual path. This will be ongoing until the mass consciousness reaches a level of loving kindness and compassion that will tip the scales for a mass manifestation of the virtues of humanity in the physical reality of the Third Dimension. Indeed, that is what we are attempting to create, the Beings of Light, with the help of our human associates.

Loving Criticism

Now, I know that I have been critical of the organized religions on your world in my current writings with you. However, I saw this as necessary for the reader, in order to clear the air, so that the truth of the matter might be openly considered. I am not, The Seth Entity in these writings is not, some kind of doomsayer attempting to sway the minds of humans to some nefarious path. My critique of your institutions and your behaviors as a collective of humans, is done for not only your own good, but for mine as a Higher Dimensional being in service to Earth at this time. I point out the fallacies in your thinking and the negative attributes of your churches and other institutions, in what I hope is a loving fashion. We who no longer have physical bodies, the Light Bodies, are in service to you and we have only love to give. It is this love I am certain, that is felt by readers of the material who truly get the messages I am attempting to convey. I wish to educate and inspire you, much as a loving coach or school teacher would. These are the personality aspects I am transmitting my energies through at this time.

Control and Submission

As I promised you in an earlier chapter, I will speak of matters related to control and submission. We have already discussed your tendency as humans to cede control - your very powerful energies of creation - to other humans, to those in power. This is a natural thing for you to do my friend, so you need not feel embarrassed. "The authorities," meaning parents, teachers, employers, religious leaders, politicians, scientists and even movie actors, have encouraged you to give up your power, what you may also refer to as "personal power." There is your dynamic - the authority pledges to provide you with protection, usually from "the other," or to provide you with subtle gifts, in exchange for your allegiance. In this contract, you give up your rights as an empowered human. You pretend that you are without power and need the security of the family group, or the scholastic group, or the employment group etc. etc. etc. It is always the same scenario: the authority usurps the power of the common one over time, usually at first with these promises of safety, of sanctuary. Do you see why we create the Ritual of Sanctuary at the beginning of this book? This we do to remind you that it is within YOU that you will find your security, your sanctuary. Within you is where it has always been. You have the power to create this state of sanctuary with your powerful thoughts and emotions.

And now it is necessary to create another ritual. This one will be a ritual of taking power - taking back your power that has been ceded, perhaps too hastily, to authorities.

Experiment - Ritual of Power
Hypothesis: in collaboration with your energy personality you may take back your power

To take back your power is a very healthy thing to do for a human quite used to "hiding" within the security of groups. This is not a power "over" but a power "with," you see - a power shared with all other incarnated humans beings. You will be reminded that you are first an individual Soul within a physical body. You-the-Soul are at the center of your physical and non-physical worlds. This cosmic center of your world is all-powerful. Though it appears that you are perhaps simply a tiny voice within a very large chorus, on a Soul level you know that you have only "pretended" to have this small voice. You had no intention of giving up your power permanently.

Let me digress on this point for a moment… in the reincarnational drama of your life, there is much pretending. The ego loves to pretend that life is a certain way and that interesting and dramatic events are occurring. If it were not for the ego's excellent dramatic skills in diverting your attention from the TRUE reality beneath the facade, you would not believe with all your heart in the camouflage reality in which you live. So it is healthy and necessary, to a degree, to believe in the fantasies and pretendings that make up your moment-to-moment existence. However, if you are to awaken, you may have to dispense with the comforting stories of your physical reality. Now that is not to say that you must surrender ALL of the physical trappings of your Personal Reality. That is not advisable and indeed that is not possible for most of you.

To take back your power requires some personalized, empowered imagery. Perhaps you can remember when you experienced your power being ceded to authorities. Perhaps you can remember feeling diminished. Perhaps you remember feeling that it was necessary to be a part of the group. If so, it should be easy to create your ritual. Simply consider the opposites of these feelings and these images.

So just as I asked you to consider your personal feelings relative to a subtle emotion of peace and security, I now ask you to consider those ideas, images and emotions relative to the idea of "taking back power." And again, it is a good idea to write down what comes to your mind. Draw pictures of the images you see in your mind. Consolidate these mental constructs into one image or emotion that virtually resonates with personal empowerment. If you feel it would help, you might create a symbolic piece of jewelry to wear or create a statement to repeat to yourself that infers the empowering ideas and images for You-the-Soul.

Now as an example: let us suppose you are experiencing a sense of disempowerment with regards to your family. This may be a long-standing condition for you, as it is with many of your contemporaries. Though you are now an adult, your parents or other family members may treat you as though you are still a child. You ceded your power to these family members when you were a child and possibly reinforced this dynamic throughout your life to "keep peace" within the group, to be a part of the family collective, in effect saying, "I am not powerful enough, I am not worthy enough to participate in the family and have my words valued.

Let these others, the authorities, run the show, and I shall reside in the background." Then as you grew to adulthood, you used this template of creation to create your roles in other groups: in school, in social groups, at work, and so on. The single template has served to create for you a lifetime of subservience to authority. You have become this "small voice" within every group thereafter.

Conduct Your Ritual of Sanctuary

You are now creating a different template for the creation of personal realities. It may be "the opposite" of the template you have been using since childhood. Now create your relaxed state. It should only take a few moments. You may connect it to snapping your fingers or gesturing with your facial expressions in some way, so that you need only to snap your fingers or gesture and instantly you are relaxed and ready for the experiment. When you are relaxed, consider your chant, imagery, piece of art, manifesto or other focusing object. Remember, it must have the capacity to elicit confidence and a sense of personal power. As you experiment with this in mind, the ritual will grow stronger and more potent. When it has become habitual, you may bring it with you and perform it mentally in the field whenever you experience disempowerment or abuse in physical reality. You are then recreating reality through a new filter and you will perceive and create empowered physical realities thereafter. **Findings** - Document your findings. Does the hypothesis need to be changed to reflect findings over time?

Experiment - SimeTime Salon
Hypothesis: you may meet with other seth entity counterparts within non-linear time

In our first book, Mark proposed in his introduction a meeting of Seth Counterparts within the spacious present moment of your shared Simultaneous Lives. I realize that this would seem to fly in the face of everything that has been taught to you in your schools. Yet remember what I have been suggesting to you about authorities and institutions. In your awakening, which is currently well underway, you will be given the opportunity many times to reformat and reconstitute your core beliefs about yourself and your world. You may do this reformation with your imagination. In this example, the last experiment of this current book, I am asking you to take a very courageous step forward into the unknown reality. I am asking you to demonstrate to yourself, Dear Reader, that you can achieve contact and communications with others such as yourself - other Seth Entity Counterparts - by simply affirming your intention to do so, here in your current Moment Point - your Point of Power. You may rely on all of the findings culled from the previous experiments.

It may help to have an underlying attitude of playfulness here. You are having fun with your imagination, just as you may have done countless times when you were a child.

Conduct Your Ritual Of Sanctuary

Now relax yourself using your most effective methods. When you are experiencing a relaxed state of consciousness, with the metaphor of the radio dial in mind, tune the dial to that state of consciousness of Simultaneous Time in which you may sense your physical counterparts. Have the intention that you will make contact, just as you have had the intention to accomplish other research goals in the previous experiments. Of course, you may ask for assistance from your Energy Personality. Now you may be presented with data for interpretation by your Inner Senses. It may come to you in various sensory forms. You may see images that are quite familiar, as if you have seen these faces many times, perhaps in dreams. You may hear sounds from other environments, other locales on your Earth. If you feel that you may take notes into a recorder or onto the pages of your journal without disrupting what you are experiencing, do so. Again, you may have the overall sense that you are making it all up. Of course, you are indeed doing so, but no less and no more than you are making up your Personal Reality Field. When you feel as though you have learned enough from the experiment, gradually come to full sensory aware-ness in physical reality.

Findings - Document your findings. Now the "after effects" of this final experiment may include "coinci-dental" meetings with your Seth Entity Counterparts as you go about your daily activities. You will know them when you see them. I am quite confident that you will achieve great success in these sojourns into the non-physical reality.

EPILOGUE

Into the Field

Knowing what is the right thing to do under the circumstances at hand, this is the key to right living for you. In this book I have suggested methods for contacting your Guides so that they may help you and indeed GUIDE you. It is then a matter of performing your contact rituals prior to communication or simply relying on an interior signal that you are ready for contact. Either way, the contact is surely made and you may use these invaluable resources - these divine intermediaries - to guide you throughout the day.

In conclusion, if you Dear Reader choose to take these messages to the world, you may be met by the nay-sayers. I will say to you exactly what I say to Mark when he is confronted by those under the influence of negative energies: "Use the techniques I have taught you and use the information you have gathered in your findings from experimentation, and transform the angry, fearful images and thoughts into the loving compassion and confidence that will sustain you." Now this is the true test of the Scientist of Consciousness: have you created your personal Ritual of Sanctuary? Have you conducted your experiments and documented your findings in a journal or other form? Have you personalized those parts of your findings that can assist you in your day-to-day learning experiences as a Soul? If you have done all this, then the nay-sayers can be met with ease. For you are indeed upon your spiritual path: assessing each moment in a positive way, exercising your free will by choosing the most auspicious of the probable behaviors before you and then acting for the most loving manifestation of all. You are becoming fully-realized and adequate for the challenges of multi-dimensional experience. You are using, my friend, the tools you have discovered, and you are gaining proficiency by venturing into the field of exploration that is your own ongoing sacred life.

QUESTIONS AND ANSWERS WITH SETH

Book Two

Seth I just wanted to continue our discussion regarding Book Two and what it will include.

Yes Mark, The Next Chapter... the segment on your Inner Senses... I want to make that essay an interactive exercise. Now, I will ask the reader to put down the book and attempt to feel and sense these Inner Senses. In a way, you have done this many times before as a child. The imagination is what powers these senses. Now you might say, "Then it is all just make believe." And I would say you were quite correct. However, in the surest sense, all in your reality is make believe, in that it is born in the collective imaginations of all of you. You decide, as a group, what you will believe into reality. You all manifest your thoughts collectively along agreed-upon rules and "specifications," for want of a better word. This is done primarily in the dream state. So you literally, as a group, dream your world into becoming and then experience it upon awakening. Yet in actuality,

201

your waking world is also a dream state. You just believe it is more "real" than your nighttime experiences and so you do indeed experience it as more real. However, both are equally valid states of consciousness. Both are equally real. Both have real consequences. Both follow their own evolutionary paths.

Now Mark, the essays in The Next Chapter will include experiments in consciousness exploration: the idea that the reader can become a true Scientist of Consciousness, using their own perceptions and senses as instruments. Naturally these instruments, continuing the analogy or metaphor, will of necessity have to have their lenses cleansed. Beliefs, images, thoughts that are of a judgmental quality will have to be wiped away. Ego-identified thoughts of a negative nature will have to be cleansed from these senses, these instruments, before they can give you a true picture of what you are witnessing. This is in essence the Soul's perspective and though I do not mean to challenge the reader too much with these phrases, I think we should continue to describe these processes and concepts for what they indeed are - spiritual ideas, the world of the human Soul. There have been some questions lately regarding the use of words such as Soul and spirit. In your world they do have religious undertones. Yet religion does not own these words and it would be a good thing I believe to take back your words, take back your thoughts, empower yourselves, re-spiritualize yourselves by redefining your beliefs about and ideas about spirituality and what it entails. With my First Subject and her mate, *(In these new writings, Seth refers to his First Subject in the feminine. mf)* it was fairly cut and dried; matters of the spirit were not discussed; they were not "scientific." Now with this current project I am asking you to redefine what a scientist is and does. The scientists of the future will, as I have said, use the instruments of their perceptions to study and recreate their world. This is the way it will be and so you may as well get a head start on your fellow humans. Then you can teach them what you have learned.

The Lost Outline

Seth, I'm happy I found that first session of ours that I put into a different directory. You laid out the future sessions nicely in that one.

Yes, the introductory material. The book The Next Chapter will comprise for the main part, discussions on the EP and the 4D: the Energy Personality and how to contact it and establish ongoing communications and the Fourth Dimension, how to contact it, develop one's etheric vision and use one's Inner Senses to enable one to remain IN it. As you have suggested before, this natural demarcation of book boundaries suggests the macro and the microcosm. As above, so below etc. etc. etc. Now Mark, we are elaborating in this second book, on material I created with my First Subject in

The Magical Approach and some other sections of past written manuscripts. You are well aware of these passages, as you are keenly interested in the magical aspects of my teaching. So we will knowingly include some of these terms from your occult tradition and perhaps explain any differences I see in the terms and emphasize the truly magical nature of mankind's existence on Earth. Now Mark I know you think of "mankind" the term as being unnecessarily sexist. Include the term in our collaborations or exclude it if you wish. Oftentimes I think it is the perfect description for what I am trying to convey to you. However, since the new material will be transmitted through you, perhaps these phrases and descriptions will fall by the wayside naturally, in the course of events as we create book material.

OK Seth, I'm perfectly happy to just act as a conduit as much as possible, though I do see the value in creating material that everyone can read without these words that can make some people put the book down.

I understand you perfectly Mark.

Seth Websites

Seth, what do you think of all these websites claiming to be authorities on your words?

Mark, I am flattered that anyone still cares. Let us be honest, after years of offering advice, I am honored that so many still remember. Now that is not to say that some are obviously on "ego trips," and you know how that rankles me. Suffice it to say Mark, that our work will come to be acknowledged by most of these people. It is undeniable is it not? I am who I say I am and that is just that. Now with you as my voice we will meet them in the lecture halls and in the metaphysical bookstores and on the streets of your great cities. We will let them know that I have returned and I am again encouraging humans to "clean up your act" and move forward in your evolution. Some will not want to hear this message. These are the ones who need to hear it the most. Some are masquerading as authorities who do not live by their words. It will be a "healing," educational experience for these people to mend their ways and move forward.

Your idea *(a thought that just crossed my mind that Seth apparently picked up on. mf)* that there is energy in my words, that the book has power on the subtle levels, is a sound one. So what we must do is get the books into the hands of people who will appreciate it. They will come to the inevitable conclusion that I have returned and they will loosen their defenses.

The ego, Mark, as I have said on countless occasions over the past two years, thinks it is in charge here in this timeframe. Yet look at what an ego-driven culture - the U.S.A. - has created. The rest of the world fears you. They do not trust you. You are the untouchable country. Quite a

205

turnaround for the "mightiest nation in the world." As a nation, the U.S.A. must take its lessons seriously and be humbled. Otherwise you will be destroyed. You will destroy yourselves. This is happening now. Your country is falling apart from within. You will see as your presidential race progresses that there is great discord across your land. People are rising up. The visionaries that I spoke of in the 9/11 book are coming forward to lead you. Your leaders, however, will not let go of the reins of power gently. They will hold on as though their very lives depend upon it, for they do. Your leaders have fallen under the influence of the Dark Forces and if they do not relinquish their stranglehold on your great nation and the world, they will be removed by the Forces of Light, pure and simple. Now this is as much as I can say about this issue currently. It is just to give you a taste of what is in store for you in the creation of Books Two and Three. This is how it feels Mark, to channel Seth. How do you feel?

It feels good. It's like being inspired really. Let's do this regularly.

We shall. Good day.

Telepathic Network

Seth could you please comment on The Telepathic

Network you have described that supports our created realities? I'm asking for an image or metaphor that could help our readers understand the concept.

Briefly… give me a moment. Layers, dimensions, holographs, grids, nested realities… all of these concepts may be used to <u>represent,</u> but only in a very superficial sense, what I am describing to you as The Telepathic Network. For the concept, the divine concept, is beyond description. When you are a regular visitor to the upper dimensions, you will be able to experience the multidimensionality of the network. That is why I am attempting to bring you and our readers along on this journey, so that the telepathic reality will be more than merely an intellectual concept.

Now everything in your reality, I repeat, is conscious, sentient, self-reflective, ALIVE. Every atom is telepathic, therefore, and every atom knows, in a holographic sense, everything about every other atom in the created Universe. So there is this mutually-supportive relationship between each and every atom. Again, you may also speak of my CUs in this way. Indeed, atoms are merely another word for my CUs a little further along on the manifestation trajectory of Reality Creation. Subjectively you may have already experienced this divine relationship as you have conducted your experiments upon reading this book. So the knowing is beyond words but well within the grasp of experiencing in the moment. We will have very much more to say about this network in the next book in this series. I trust this description will suffice until the next project is completed.

Lemurians

Seth, you asked me to remind you to make further comments on the Lemurian civilization for the Q&A Section. Would you do so now?

The Lemurians, Mark, are literally within your reach every moment of your waking and dreaming lives. They may be approached through rituals of contact, just as we have been describing in this book. Now you may have noticed that it is this ritualistic approach conducted time and time again with a purposeful intent that creates these opportunities for contacting the Etheric Beings, such as Beings of Light and your other spiritual counterparts. It is quite the same with contacting the Lemurian citizens. One might best describe these relationships as communications with one's Allies or Familiars. Just as the various non-physical Entities that are watching over you may be entrusted to guide you and assist in your awakening, these inhabitants of the underworld may be enlisted to guide you within their domains. The various visualized routes to this realm are to be found in gardens, down into the Earth via visualized self-created holes in the ground, and so on. Ask for contact and guidance in your meditations and diligently look for opportunities in your waking and dreaming worlds for contact. When you have achieved contact, ask for specific guidance as to what you may be allowed to see and experience in their world. Honesty, compassion and integrity are your watchwords in these and all attempts at contact with the non-physical beings.

Negative Entity

Seth, can you describe a Negative Entity for us?

Yes Mark, we shall have that discussion. As I have described to you previously, All That Is is the creative source for all realities. You are a spin-off of All That Is, and you are currently, as are your contemporaries, learning your lessons within your individual Personal Reality Fields. Now there is a greater, more expansive field of interaction in which you and your current timeframe inhabitants experience your lives. This context we might call the Spiritual or Etheric Realm of your planet. This realm is inhabited by Higher Dimensional Beings. These beings, including the Beings of Light, are created out of consciousness as it is embodied within human Souls experiencing lives on your Earth and elsewhere. Now, just as positive, loving influences of consciousness create Beings of Light, the negative, hateful, destructive influences of consciousness - what you might call the opposite of the positive influences - create the Nefarious Entities, the Negative Energy Beings we have noted in our two books. It is a logical premise here Mark. Consciousness creates realities and the beings that inhabit them.

Currently, the Negative Entities have a hold on your leaders, particularly in the West. This would seem obvious but I shall digress… murder in the form of the individual taking of lives by humans on your streets and in your homes, is a negative act, a Violation. The collective taking of lives by groups of people, such as your military in their excursions into foreign lands, is a collective Violation. Were your leaders in league with the Beings of Light - a relationship we are attempting to create at this time - you would not be experiencing the negative realities of war, collapsing economies, hatred for the poor and disabled etc. etc. etc. I will end the description now, and allow you and the reader to fill in the blanks. You know what you must do to change this state of affairs. We are giving the reader the tools to make the changes with these books we are creating at this time.

Subjects in the Last Twenty Years

Seth, who have you spoken through in the last twenty years since your First Subject's death?

Yes Mark, I can answer the question fairly specifically. Give me a moment… Your unraveling of the thread regarding Huxley (*Aldous Huxley mf*) is "timely." Now, my First Subject did indeed pick up the "line" almost immediately after the death of

210

Huxley, yet Huxley was not the only listener on the "party line." There were and are countless participants in this communication network. Yet only a few, such as yourself, have succeeded in capturing and publishing the information. For the last twenty years, in your timeframe, many authors have written books from my communications with them, though they did not regard their writing process as "Seth-based," they simply felt they were creatively writing from their own "genius." This is how it should be and how it has been for many years on your planet. To be specific, look at your New Age books and see those that seem to be Seth-based. Use your intuition and you will see that The Seth Entity is raising-up the consciousness of humankind, partly through the publication of these books "anonymously." Now Mark, you are the first writer to carry my books to market under the auspices of The Seth Entity since the death of my First Subject. And you can tell anyone who asks, that I said this.

(Note: Seth seems to be implying that Aldous Huxley was in communication with The Seth Entity. mf)

Reader's Question on Urantia

Seth do you want to answer the reader's question on Urantia? What do you think about it?

Mark, I will answer the question at this time. The material that the reader of the 9/11 book refers to is important literature for many people. It is channeled material from what

211

you would call "extra-terrestrial" origins. Now, Biblical ideas and characters are used as the starting points for discussions on the nature of your Third-Dimensional existence and beyond. As I explained in the 9/11 book, I am not of the extra-terrestrial nature. However, I feel that I can comment on this phenomenon. These entities are as real as I am. If you accept The Seth Entity as a teacher and educator, you could easily accept these teachings as just as valid, though perhaps appealing to a different aspect of humanity. Beings of Light are stepping-up their communications with and influence on humanity at this time. The expression, "to take what you need and leave the rest," is wholly adequate advice for seekers of divine information during this critical period of learning on your planet. Now I will elaborate somewhat on a previous comment I made in the 9/11 book…the so-called "extraterrestrials" are closer than you think. As I said previously, if one were to think of inter-dimensional rather than extra-terrestrial, one would be closer to the fact.

Native Americans

Can you answer my mother's question about the Native Americans? She wants you to comment on Native Americans as "the first people." Where did the Native Americans come from?

Mark I am never far away. Yes, the Native American people do call themselves the first people and for good reason. They were, like the other indigenous peoples of the world, originally brought to Earth from other star systems, most notably Sirius. Now remember, it is also true that the whole of humanity has their origins in other star systems and solar systems, but it is the aboriginal peoples, such as the Native Americans, who remember this connection, for they have kept the story alive over many, many generations, through story, song and mental communication or telepathy. Also remember here Mark that concepts such as "genealogy" and the "family tree" lose meaning when one considers that Souls incarnate into particular families for purposes of learning specific lessons. In other words, you have been a Native American, and many, many other nationalities in your many journeys into physical incarnation. Your mother has also. You are brought together in this current timeframe to learn your lessons within your particular family unit. You know what those lessons are. They are acutely obvious to all of you. When you make The Transition into your Home Dimension, you may choose another family to be born into, possibly joining members of your current family in different bodies to continue your lessons, or you will move on to the "higher" dimensional realms. I hope I am not boring you, but this is the truth about the family tree. It has infinitely more branches and roots than you suppose.

Thanks Seth.

You are welcome, Mark, and wish your mother a Happy Mother's Day.

Lectures

Can you speak to the idea that you and I will be able to fill lecture halls with people who will be eager to hear you speak through me?

The answer to your question is yes, if you create the network for the manifestation. This simply means putting the world out that Seth has returned, as I have stated before. You WILL attract my fans from all over the world to come to your lectures. You needn't have fears that I will desert you. We should practice on a smaller scale with me coming through and speaking to groups of 10, 20 or 30 people. Then you will be prepared for the lecture halls of the world, as I have mentioned to you several times before. Have confidence and continue creating books.

Seth's First Subject

Has your First Subject embarked upon another life? Are you teaching her in an incarnation in this timeframe? What is my relationship to her?

My First Subject has not embarked upon another reincarnational venture since her last passing. She is in her

Home Dimension doing what she likes best: studying, writing, creating. She is a gifted Entity and loves to use her talents in the creative arts. As I have said to you before, I am still her teacher and mentor. We are continually engaged in our collaborative efforts as Scientists of Consciousness. Some of the projects involve you, for that matter. We may, if you approve, attempt a three-way communication between my First Subject, myself and you Mark. It's easy for you to engage in the two-way exchange with me; I'm sure it will be just as easy to do the three-way exchange, once I can fine-tune the energies to permit this. All it takes is your free will offering to participate.

I accept. It sounds exciting. Could this be book material?

Yes Mark, it will be exciting and worthy of its own book. Perhaps we shall name it Project First Subject or something similar. Now to answer your question regarding your relationship with my First Subject... You Mark are a simultaneous life in The Seth Entity constellation of lives, which includes my Second Subject and others in your timeframe who are still in the physical body. You will meet other fellow Seth Entity members in the future as you take my messages to the world. You will know them immediately. I will remind you. You are a member of this brother and sisterhood and from the commonality you will band together to help in the remaking of your world through media - loving media. As I said in dictation, you are the Vanguard and you

215

will lead the new visionaries into leadership roles in all of your Earthly institutions. Now, you will do this humbly with the confidence of knowing what is right behavior in any particular moment. I will be your Guide personally and the other Beings of Light will guide their associates in your Third-Dimensional world. Together we will comprise an unstoppable movement of "do-gooders" and radical, loving transformers of consciousness and thus systems. This has been a long-winded answer, but I must prepare you for the good work ahead. You are wise to move toward a healthier lifestyle. You will need high energy for this new career of yours.

Microwave Energies

Carol Joy asks, "Can Seth tell us about microwave energies, the kind emitted by communications hardware that is installed on hill tops and telephone poles so that people can use their cell phones? Do these energies have an effect on the people who live near them, work by them, or drive through them? Also, do cell phones damage the user's brain?"

Now... the microwave energies that you speak of can be harmful if a human is in the path of transmission and they are close to the source. Obviously, the greater the distance from the source, the less harm done, but there are effects on the human system at all levels of interaction with these microwaves. Without getting into details, these powerful energies "burn" tissue, human tissue. If one is driving their automobile through the broadcasted "spray" of the transmission stream, one is protected somewhat from the effects on the body. If one is walking through the stream, one is not protected, however, the effects are diffuse on the body, in most cases. The entire body takes the brunt of the burning effect and so one does not feel the tissue destruction. This destruction is similar in many ways to the effects of nuclear fallout, yet nuclear fallout is far more harmful and I have noted in my last volume that your world is virtually immersed in a radioactive cloud that is the cause of many of your diseases. Now your microwave energies can also cause mutations in the human body, and they do so over the long term, just as in the radioactive effects on humans.

Your question regarding the effects on users of cell phones can be answered similarly. Users of these phones will be harmed according to their resistance to these energies. Children would be harmed the most, healthy adults the least, but there will always be some damage to tissues from using these phones directly next to the skull.

Mormon Religion

JF asks, "In the Mormon religion it is claimed that Joseph Smith found golden tablets and that he communicated with God who told him that the Mormons were the chosen people of God. Is this true?"

There is a saying in your culture that "one should never discuss religion or politics with a friend, for you will surely destroy that relationship." With that in mind, I will delicately attempt an answer to your question (humorously). Your church leader Joseph Smith no doubt experienced a revelation - a deeply personal and powerful encounter with the spiritual side of humankind. These encounters are often experienced in terms of magnificent visions and uplifting and righteous emotions, sometimes including the feelings that one has been "chosen" to share the revelations with others, and perhaps lead them on a quest for higher consciousness.

Your Joseph Smith did indeed, like many before and after him, experience a "revelation," or deep understanding of the nature of his reality and the nature of his Soul Self. His interpretation of this vision was made through his individual psyche and belief system and so the revelation bore the major aspects of his personality. Now, another person, let us say a more modern individual, one from the year 2004, having a similar revelation, would also interpret it through the filter of their own psyche and belief system and possibly come up with something completely different than gold tablets and a mandate regarding the "chosen people." The context of the times and personality idiosyncrasies mark these revelations and their interpretations, in other words. Also I must add that ANY human has the potential for experiencing revelatory material. ANY human can experience contact with their Soul Self. That is indeed what this current book is about, and that is where the experimentation hopefully leads. This is not to negatively critique the religious movement Joseph Smith founded, by any means. I am simply suggesting that the revelatory material he accessed can be accessed by anyone, given the right circumstances and openness to spiritual matters.

(My ears were burning as I took Seth's dictation on this question. I saw the obvious similarities between our work and the work of Joseph Smith, as well as the visions of my ancestor that I described earlier. I am inspired by my connections to these larger-than-life characters, including Seth. mf)

Earth Changes

MC wants to know, "How are the earthquakes, volcanic activity and strange weather phenomena related to the subjects you talk about in your latest books?"

Yes Mark, we covered that question in Book One, but I will answer the question again with a particular emphasis. The weather in any particular area of your world is the result of the thoughts, images and emotions held in the collective consciousness of that area. All creates the weather: rocks, trees, microbes, humans - everything in your reality has consciousness, and the collective, local mass consciousness is expressed in the particular weather patterns of that area. Now, in a private session, if you remember, I spoke of the poetic justice of an episode of extremely strange weather occurring in a part of the U.S. that was noted for its extremely inhumane political views and anti-human religious views. This episode of strange weather demonstrated perfectly how your thoughts of negativity swirl up around you to create negative weather events. I trust that this short explanation will satisfy our reader.

Holograms

Seth, can you talk about these brief "holograms" you have been sending to me lately?

Mark, yes, these are momentary Holographic Inserts I send to you to illustrate a subject we are or will be discussing. They are quite brief so that you will not be completely drawn into them, as you would be if they were much longer than a fraction of a second in your time. The pleasure element is included so you will notice the content and remember it. Now, in our earlier discussions on the subject of Holographic Inserts *(Book One. mf)*, I described how they are used to create the impression that something is happening on a mass consciousness level that in fact is not truly occurring in your reality. These momentary Holographic Inserts I use to illustrate the dictation or teaching in the moment. Many of us in the higher realms use these techniques when we wish to stress a particular point or when the subject requests inspiration by using their free will to ask for it. Obviously, we do not willy-nilly fire off Holographic Inserts to control or in any way adversely affect a subject. These are benign, loving constructs, Mark. One can easily sense their connection to the substrata of ecstatic emotion I am often describing to you.

Accepted and Rejected Fields

How are your concepts of Accepted or Rejected Fields of Reality related to the "magical approach" you wrote about in an earlier manuscript?

Now Mark, you are beginning to see the seamless connections between my concepts. In essence, all is one, and this includes human consciousness and these various levels or states we have been discussing. So for practical purposes - for the practical magician (humorously) - one learns how to accept the impossible as possible, as an Accepted Field of Reality. It's all done with CUs again, through one's intent. This intent - or perhaps Divine Will, if you are spiritually-minded - simply means one co-creates with All That Is on a conscious level. Your intent then has the full creative powers of the natural world behind it. The great altruistic creators of humankind know this. They know about Divine Will.

Can you give me an example of one of my Rejected Fields of Reality that would help me if I could transform it into an Accepted Field of Reality?

Mark, what are you afraid of? You have now and you have had for a number of years the tools to create the reality you dream of. What are you afraid of? Now, perhaps I should ask, "What are you afraid of that is <u>also</u> something you greatly desire?" For it is here within these conflicting belief systems that your answers lie. Now, if I may be so bold, and you are giving me telepathic permission to go on... you do much <u>talking</u> about your need for prosperity, your home and land. Yet Mark, if you examine your beliefs and their subsequent behaviors, you may see that you are going at cross-purposes with yourself with regards to creating your home and land. You are being timid in these instances of "asking the universe" for what you want and you are also asking from a place of fear. In essence you are saying, "I want a nice house on some beautiful acreage," at the same time you say to yourself "I don't deserve this," "It takes too much effort to get this," etc. etc. etc.

So do you see that your self-effacing, negative comments to yourself are more powerful than your statements that you wish to have a house and land? Cross-purposes Mark. Your task, and I am sure, many of the readers will have similar tasks, is to charge your self-comments with positive, generative energy and then actively PARTICIPATE IN THEIR MANIFESTATION. Timidity is not for magicians Mark.

Take back your power from your employer, from your government, from your church, from your friends and family and use it to create your house and land.

As you take back your power and you begin to realize your innate goodness and you begin to live from love and confidence, what you fear will become an Accepted Field of Reality for you. You fear prosperity. You assume that the wealthy are somehow tainted by their money. You fear that you may become tainted also if you were to acquire wealth and so you create just enough to live on, just enough to remain poor, just enough to avoid facing your prosperity "issues." I am done for now on this subject. I hope you forgive me for being blunt.

You know I do. I asked for it.

Etheric Vision

Can you comment on Etheric Vision? How do we experiment with it? How can we develop it?

Mark, yes, the term Etheric Vision refers to the use of the physical vision receptors to perceive the Fourth Dimension. I distinguish it from the Inner Senses generally, which are more emotionally experienced. Now, your descriptions of your holograms I sent you are very much like descriptions of Etheric Vision. The Fourth Dimension favors pastel colors in a sort of dreamy landscape. Many of your New

Age artists have captured the essence of Etheric Vision. As you begin to accept this faculty and you focus your intent on learning how to see your world through this perspective, the momentary glimpses will become longer in duration, until eventually you will be able to turn on and turn off your etheric vision as easily as you can now open and close your eyes to see or to close off your physical vision.

Negative or Benign Energy

How do I tell if I am receiving communications from a negative energy or a benign energy?

Mark, now this is an excellent question and one I am sure our readers would be interested in having answered. As we have covered in an earlier part of this work, protection rituals are an important prelude to your psychic investigations. So develop your own techniques and implement them each time you voyage to the subtle levels. And as I have also mentioned on many occasions, and please underline this Mark, <u>negative energy seeks out fear and anxiety</u>. The Negative Entities feed off of your negative emotions. So perhaps in addition to surrounding yourself with light and other rituals, one should intentionally clear one's emotional space, replacing fear and anger with love and confidence etc. etc. etc. As for recognizing negative energies when you are meditating or even while you are going about your daily life in your existence, the advice is similar: if you are feeling anxious, fearful and angry, you are under the influence of the Negative Entities and you should immediately take action by clearing your Emotional Body.

Atlantean Hologram

Can you discuss the Atlantean hologram?

Now Mark, you have free will to do as you wish in the evolution of your Soul. You asked for a hologram yesterday and I attempted to present one to your consciousness, but the timing was not right. I did present you with some images of Atlantean concepts that you interpreted into your dream symbolism. Now it was a literal symbol though Mark - humans connected in a grid framework and cultivating power from this. It is a symbolic image also in that it can represent the power of people when they are united, "combined" in common cause. Your interpretation of the image was correct for your consciousness and it is appropriate for the Atlantean culture. Yet see how Book Two can be connected to the image also. You will be creating a network of people who will be creating power collectively: political, social, economic etc. Also this group will be setting the stage for the development of the telepathic/brain power network of the Atlantean culture that exists past, present and future.

The Maitreya

Is Benjamin Crème's Maitreya the World Teacher you described in your earlier writings, the one who will come and bring the Christ teachings?

Mark, The Christ is actively collaborating with <u>many</u> Masters in your world today. I would not single out just one, however. It is highly ethnocentric and ego-perceptive to think that one Master will bring in the new vibrations and changes that will usher humanity into the Fourth Dimension. There are many Masters and each has their part to play. Specializing in only one can skew the message. Better to seek a plurality of spiritual guidance from as many as one can. As I said, I am a messenger from All That Is in service to mankind and I do specialize in Western humanity. There are others in service to Earth that teach and are in service to Eastern humanity, and so on. You Mark have sought out the teachings of indigenous shamans and masters of the occult arts. This works for you. This is the rich bed upon which you are building your spiritual platform from which you will transmit my teachings, other teachings, and your own synthesis in time.

Atlantean Myth

Do you want to elaborate on the Atlantean material for the Book?

Mark, the Atlantis "myth" has a rich history in your dimension. It is a highly romanticized history, in that your Hollywood movies have created for mass consumption, images based upon typical Hollywood concepts such as romantic love, good vs evil, the "dangers" inherent in sophisticated technology, and so on. Your stories and movies portray Atlantis in much the same way that your storytellers and movie-makers portray any "historical" era, whether it be biblical, medieval or prehistoric. So humankind, particularly Westerners, do not understand the true story of Atlantis. Ironically, this story is part of humankind's spiritual heritage that has been buried under layers of religious dogma, incorrect thinking and fear. As you as a race of human beings are brought into the light, an understanding of these proto-cultures will be brought into your comprehension. You Mark can anticipate the connections between your Soul Self and Atlantis to be understood and appreciated very soon in your timeframe.

Rosicrucian Saying

Seth, would you comment on MC's question regarding the Rosicrucian saying, "One can achieve immortality in two ways: by having children and by seeking and attaining enlightenment?"

Yes Mark, I shall answer the question as best I can. Now, strictly speaking, you are all - meaning humankind - already immortal. You are each composed of godstuff: aware matter that is boundless and eternal. When you make The Transition into your Home Dimension after the physical death of your human body, each cell as it degrades - or should I say - is transformed into something else, it RETAINS the memories and experiences of the life of Mark. In this way, you are infinitely immortal. Now additionally, all of your Simultaneous Lives past, present and future are also immortal. Everything in your Third-Dimensional timeframe is immortal, it simply appears that substances - including those of which you are made - age and die. Those who attain "enlightenment," as you call it, are simply better informed on this subject than others. The enlightened KNOW that they are immortal. Perhaps they have experienced a timeless moment - a moment when they have received divine information that helped unlock the mysteries for them personally. Anyone can theoretically have children, yet does that make one aware that they are immortal? I would think that would depend on the state of one's evolution as a Soul.

Religion and Control of Women

Can you shed some light on MC's question regarding religion as patriarchal control and subjugation of women?

Your friend is quite right. Historically, the female gender on your planet has been marginalized via the social structures of your world's societies. Now, this has been the case across the board, in the majority of cultures currently and in your very distant past, as you perceive it. Again, this is a perception. On the outside, it "appears" that women have been done a disservice at the hands of the male figureheads in the world's religions. Yet if you have been listening to me at all over the years, you know that women AND men experience their lessons on Earth for the greater experience of All That Is. Some of these experiences are perceived as negative, some positive and some the difference between.

The journeys into physical existence are cyclical. For your perceived past you have been witnessing the cycle of male dominance in your cultures. The other side of the cycle, however, reveals female dominance, in a complementary fashion. Now these instances of matriarchal power on your planet are, for the most part, expressed in probable realities. So those of you who are entranced by the ebb and flow of consensus reality, do not witness the probable roads not taken. Yet one can experience these unseen timelines if one wishes to use the Inner Senses we have been discussing.

Again, All That Is, the creative source for ALL in your system and all systems, experiences every possible permutation of human experience for purposes of its own Value Fulfillment. This would include ALL probable realities, whether experienced as consensus or Personal Reality by one, many or all humans or NOT experienced in physical reality by one, many or all humans. The probable realities of which I speak are just as valid as what you would term your Personal Reality, or your "bedrock reality."

I realize it may seem unfair to some of you that your perceived world is filled with male, authoritarian religious figures. However, please realize that, for your own reasons, humankind has CHOSEN these reality constructs to be manifest as learning experiences in consensus reality. One would do well to look "behind the scenes" in your own Personal Reality Field, and see if you might discover YOUR OWN PERSONAL REASONS for creating your contribution to these manifestations. There you will find fertile ground for planting new seeds that may grow into more pertinent and pleasing Reality Constructs. And again, I repeat, where many of you contribute to this endeavor, there is the opportunity for changing the local and global manifestations to the feminine expression through your social, religious and political institutions. Do you see Mark?

I do. And I think others will also. I do believe that we may have similar questions in the future, but this is a good start.

Babyhood

Carol Joy asks, "Please expound on babyhood. What happens on a Soul level?

An excellent question from your partner, I must say. Babyhood is indeed an extremely creative stage of life in the development of the human. Since one is fresh from the home dimension, there may be lingering memories of that experience. The baby may hold full memories of the previous incarnation as well, and may be experiencing a "reliving" of past experiences while seemingly engrossed in the typical baby behaviors one notices. Now, the job of the parent, unfortunately, is usually to train the infant in the ways of the world - physical reality. And so the parents begin the task of socializing the infant. As this process continues, the baby spends so much time engaged in the training - being trained to fit into the culture - that memories of the past incarnation and the time in between lives, are quickly forgotten. It is rare that a child grows to adulthood with these precious memories intact. So the divinity of babyhood is experienced by all of you, but only for a few short months. After that, the connection is broken. The child is watched carefully to assure that they are developing "normally." And when imaginary playmates arrive, modern parents too often are fearful that the child might grow into adulthood with these characters at their side. They are mostly banished by parents, as an embarrassment. The child is then taught to let go of these primal relationships, and most do. Again, in your aboriginal cultures and some alternative communities, the baby is encouraged to be "the divine one" long into childhood. This sets the state for the development of the divine child, the magical child: being the human that lives in both the subtle and physical worlds with grace and power.

Crop Circles and Other Electromagnetic Phenomena

Seth, can you explain to our readers what you meant in one of the sessions when you said that Crop Circles were an electromagnetic phenomenon?

Yes, I shall add to that exchange. Give me a moment… Now, electromagnetism is a conscious Entity. I have spoken to you before about the consciousness of EVERY-THING in your created realities. All realities are composed of elements that are conscious and self-reflective. I realize this may be a barrier to acceptance and understanding for some of you, but it is quite true, my Dear Readers. Self-reflective, sentient, aware… each of the Consciousness Units can be so described. The Crop Circles are merely the physical manifestations of what you might term "pools" of highly creative CUs under the "direction" of the natural elements within your physical reality in your Third Dimension. This accounts for their great, harmonious and natural beauty, does it not? In a sense, your Mother Nature is the artist behind these astoundingly beautiful works of art.

You too, as the co-creators of your physical world, have a hand in these creations. This occurs, however, on a subliminal level. This may account for the proclamations by some, that they "recognize" these designs, as though they were seen in the mind's eye. So these works of art are really the products of consciousness and they are also literally conscious products (humorously), if you follow my logic here. I will leave it at that and encourage you to further your investigations of this phenomenon using your Inner Senses. This will open up to you a literal Universe of information.

Tsunami

Seth, could you comment on the tsunami that has taken so many lives recently?

Yes, I shall comment... a moment. Now as you know, the reality of the situation is this: on a Soul level, each of the "victims" of the natural event knew that they were to die. The Soul incarnates to learn lessons such as these, though the ego often seems puzzled. Therefore, questions such as, "Why did so many innocents have to die," and "Was this some sort of punishment?" arise. This is not punishment, certainly. Thousands have surrendered the physical for the etheric. They are now in their Home Dimensions. They are engaged in renewing friendships on these subtle levels and reminiscing over the past Earthly visit. This is also an Earth Changes event. Your Mother Earth has shrugged her shoulders in response to your uncaring treatment of her. And notice how the true quality of America's caring compassion is found wanting in your political circles. Now the world knows. But these Earth Changes are increasing in severity. This will continue to occur as the negative egoic energies and thoughtforms of the masses of wrong-thinking humans coalesce into weather and Earth Changes. Negativity in action, that is the most basic way to describe it. It is essential that you begin to clean up your thoughts. See how the "disaster" occurred on the West's holiest of days? This illustrates on a Soul level how far away you are in the West from the "Christian" ideals you celebrate with such gusto during the Holidays.

Dolphins and Whales

Seth, I think that a few words on dolphins and whales would be appropriate for the book. Why do so many New Age proponents revere these creatures of the deep?

The inevitable question arises from the Atlantean. A moment here as I format the reply... Now, all of God's creatures, as you call them, are better caretakers of the Earth than the human race. It is a cliche currently, however, I shall repeat it. How many whales, dolphins or other creatures have waged wars that decimated the populations of cities on your Earth. You know the answer of course. It is only man, humankind that does this. The other species are content to live their lives as they do - naturally. A second point here, the dolphins and whales in particular are very wise beings. They share multi-dimensional realities and are revered not only by your New Agers but by other humanoid peoples in other star systems. These creatures are your teachers, yet historically they have been slaughtered for product-making and in the process of fishing for other animals. Again, to be used as products. This is how it is for you and your race, Mark. Everything is a product. Even those animals that, at base, have a longer history in your world and a greater accumulated wisdom because of it. Those of you who revere these animals are in all likelihood repeating older, ancient behaviors.

As I have been mentioning to you recently, every moment of your self-created and then perceived reality is a repetition of other very similar behaviors enacted in Simultaneous Lives past, present and future. You are a dolphin lover. You are a whale lover. Remember for a moment when you have done this in other ways, here on your Earth and in other Dimensions. I would ask the dolphin and whale lovers in our readership to do the same. Much can be gained

*I think we're going to have to do a book or two or three
or four or many more to get the masses
to see the problem ...***Seth**

Seth has promised to continue to communicate with us to further the awakening of humanity. This means that there will be an ongoing source of current, inspirational messages available here at
Seth Returns Publishing.

Communications from Seth on the Awakening of Humanity
Vol I ~ 9/11: The Unknown Reality of the World $19.95
The first original Seth book in two decades.
Vol II ~ The Next Chapter in the Evolution of the Soul $15.95
The Scientists of Consciousness workbook.
Vol III
To be published in 2006 - 2007

Available by mail at:

**Seth Returns Publishing
P.O. Box 150152
San Rafael, CA 94915-0152**

Personal check or money order should include the cost of book plus $5.00 for handling and shipping in the Continental United States and Canada. Please include 7.75 % sales tax if ordering in California. You can also shop online at our website **SethReturns.com** or visit **Amazon.com.**